ACTS
OF THE APOSTLES

Other Books by August Van Ryn

Meditations in Matthew

Meditations in Mark

Meditations in Luke

Meditations in John

Ephesians: The Glories of His Grace

The Epistles of John

His Appointments

The Kingdoms of God and of Heaven

ACTS

OF THE APOSTLES

THE UNFINISHED WORK OF CHRIST

By

August Van Ryn

LONDON
PICKERING & INGLIS, Ltd.

FIRST EDITION, OCTOBER 1961

Library of Congress Catalog Card Number: 61-14601
PRINTED IN THE UNITED STATES OF AMERICA

Preface

THE BOOK of "Acts" naturally comes in order after the books of "facts"—the four Gospels. As those tell us what the Son of God did and said during His perfect life of love, His death upon the Cross, His resurrection and ascension to God's right hand in Heaven, so the book of Acts delineates the doings and the ministry of the Holy Spirit, who came into the world to abide in the saints after the Ascension of our Lord Jesus Christ.

As the Gospels unfold the life of the Saviour, so the book of Acts follows with an account of the life of the saints—lived by the power of the Spirit of God.

The book begins with the formation of the Church—at Pentecost—by the descent and the baptism of the Holy Spirit, when believers were united into one Body; and it continues on to tell of the spread of the gospel, the forming of churches from among Jews and Gentiles. It gives us the history of the early years of Christianity and the gradual development of Christian truth and practice, specially as committed to the Apostle Paul, whose labors and experiences occupy the largest part of the book.

Acts is an intensely interesting and instructive volume, and I do trust that God will use my meditations on it to make His truth clearer to some, as well as to stir us all to increased devotion to Christ and His service.

AUGUST VAN RYN

CONTENTS

PART ONE

Introduction

The Author

Although he makes no mention of his name, Luke undoubtedly is the divine instrument employed by God to write this peculiarly interesting and instructive book. Away back to the earliest centuries his authorship has been acknowledged by unbiased critics. He wrote the Gospel which we know under his name as well. Both Luke and Acts are addressed to one Theophilus and bear evident marks of similarity of style, both in the identity of language (more than 40 words found in both books are found nowhere else in the New Testament), and also in the common use of medical terms. The opening reference to a former treatise known to Theophilus clearly marks Luke as the author of both Luke and Acts.

The Theme

Luke's aim is not to write biographies of either Peter or Paul, for the history of both men is left in mid-air, but to give the history of the introduction of Christianity as it takes the place of Judaism, which for many centuries had been the God-given religion. He shows how the Church is formed and how the work of preaching the gospel of God's grace extended from Jerusalem till it reached Rome, ever going westward. He has in view the history of the Church as a whole; not the growth of local churches, but the advancement of this great New Testament mystery, promised by our Lord in John 10:16, conceived at Pentecost, and concerning which the truth was only gradually revealed and taught. The Church is such a radical and absolutely new thing, contrasted with Judaism, that the full revelation of it was given but slowly. It took years for the new believers, impregnated as they were by the teachings of Judaism, to be delivered from Jewish thinking, ceremonies, and connections.

The New Testament, as shown by F. W. Grant, is built in the form of a Pentateuch, patterned after the Pentateuch of the first five books of the Bible. The four Gospels answer to the book of Genesis, giving us the beginning of things. Exodus pictures next the book of Acts, giving the story of the "going out" of the people of God, not from physical bondage, as in their deliverance from Egypt's slavery, but from the bondage of the law, which was a servitude (a "yoke," as Peter calls it in Acts 15:10) which neither their fathers nor they were able to bear. Hence in the book of Acts grace takes the place of law, Christianity the place of Judaism. Israel nationally is set aside, because in putting their Messiah on the Cross, the nation as such finally and fully refused and rejected its King.

In contrast to this, Acts presents the gathering together of all the children of God—believing Jew and Gentile united in one Body by the Cross (Ephesians 2:16). Throughout the book of Acts the Jews are seen continually rejecting God's mercy, with the gospel going out ever more widely to the Gentiles. It begins to be preached at Jerusalem, then to Judea, to Samaria, and at last to the uttermost parts of the earth. Its reception by the Gentiles only increases Jewish hatred and opposition, and repeatedly we hear God's messengers declaring that they will turn to the Gentiles. Paul, the great apostle to the Gentiles, displaces Peter on the page of inspiration, and more than half of the book of Acts is engaged with an account of his labors far and wide, under the guidance and by the power of the Holy Spirit.

Israel is not on probation in Acts, but rather we read of its persistent attitude of ever-refusing and rejecting Christ. Away back in Matthew 23:39 the Lord Jesus told the Israelites that God had departed out of their midst, that their house was left unto them desolate, and that they were never to see the Lord again until they should say: "Blessed is He that cometh in the name of the Lord."

I do not believe that anywhere in Acts is there an offer made of Christ's reign over them as His kingdom on earth, if they would only receive Him as Saviour. Rather, their determined sin in rejecting Christ is emphasized over and over again. Peter urges his hearers to save themselves from this untoward generation, plainly intimating that, as to the nation as a whole, it had not changed its mind or its attitude towards the Christ since it had crucified its Messiah. Salvation was not offered to the nation as such, but to individuals who by faith in the Saviour would thus separate themselves from the apostate nation of Israel. Only those who repented would be saved through Christ and saved from Israel and its religion.

Peter tells them in the third chapter of Acts that the Messiah was not coming back, for Heaven was to receive Him till the times of restitution of all things (and all the Old Testament prophets plainly show that this time of restitution lies still in the future, awaiting the hour when Christ will come to reign as King). Instead of offering Israel another chance to acknowledge Christ and thus have Him set up His kingdom on earth, the gospel is preached to them (and to all that were afar off, thus including the Gentiles) for the acceptance of individual faith in Christ. Instead of Israel's being offered a second chance to own Christ as King, the apostles in their preaching charge them with unvarying hatred and rebellion. A notable example of this is in Stephen's searing indictment of the nation as recorded in Acts 7, though Stephen was not one of the apostles. He rebukes the nation for its murderous hatred, and there is not the remotest sign of another chance offered to Israel; the same holds true throughout the book of Acts.

The book closes with Paul preaching the gospel of the kingdom of God and the things concerning the Lord Jesus Christ: a clear suggestion of what still is being carried on today. The kingdom is not Christ's literal kingdom on earth, but the kingdom which one enters through new birth (John 3:5), while the believer is taught the precious things concerning the Lord Jesus Christ, so fully revealed today through the ministry of Paul, who was specially chosen to be the minister of the Church.

Into the doctrines of the Christian faith the book of Acts hardly enters, for Acts is history, not doctrine.

There is, however, a gradual development of doctrine from the forgiveness of sins to justification to the believer's position today in the Church of God, which is the Body of Christ. Many make the mistake of reading established doctrines into the book of Acts and of building erroneous conclusions as a result. Acts presents a progressive history from Judaism into Christianity, and is therefore fluid in its teaching. Today, with the full revelation of God's Word in the New Testament, Christianity is now fully established and thus Christian doctrine is now static, completely unfolded in the New Testament Epistles. Look for history in Acts, for doctrine in the Epistles, and all will prove to be perfectly consistent and harmonious.

I

The Unfinished Work of Christ

"THE FORMER treatise have I made, O Theophilus, of all that Jesus began both to do and teach"—Acts 1:1

This opening verse bids us look back to Christ's finished work, as recorded by Luke in the Gospel that bears his name, and bids us look forward by implication to His unfinished work, which He left for His servants to carry on during this day of grace, for our text says that Jesus *began* to do and teach. He laid the foundation at Calvary for His Church (Ephesians 2:20); the actual building of this Church is the privilege and responsibility of God's people, as by the Spirit's power they preach the gospel of God's grace by means of which souls are saved and built upon this foundation, laid deep and true on Calvary's cross.

The four Gospels, one of which Luke reminds Theophilus he wrote, give us the facts concerning the Person and work of Christ, and, as John 20:31 states, they are written that we might believe that Jesus is the Christ and that, believing, we might have life through His Name. Those who believe in Jesus should prove their faith by their works, so it is indeed fitting that the books of "facts" (the four Gospels), should be followed by the book of "Acts." If we truly believe in Jesus, we are going to act upon that belief; we are going to follow the example of Him who *began* to do and teach; and, when He returned to Heaven, left us down here to continue the work which He began.

The Gospels teach us that our blessed Lord finished one work, while He also left other work unfinished. In John 17:4 we hear Him say: "I have glorified Thee on the earth: I have finished the work which Thou gavest Me to do." And from His cross we listen to His triumphant shout: "It is finished" (John 19:30).

Perhaps the greatest commendation ever given by the Lord Jesus is found in Mark 14:8, where of the woman who poured ointment on His head He said: "She hath done what she could." Throughout the Gospels we notice that the Lord seldom did things which others could do as well. For instance, at Lazarus' grave he told the bystanders to take away the stone. He alone could bring the dead man back to life, but others could move the stone, and also could take off the graveclothes. So Jesus broke the five loaves and two fishes: He alone could miraculously multiply food in that astounding fashion; but the disciples could distribute the feast, and were told to do so. So today Jesus enlists every believer in His service to do what he can do; but before that He finished a work He alone could accomplish—the mighty work of redemption, and when it was so done He exclaimed: "It is finished." We speak of it naturally as the "finished work of Christ." In simple terms: Christ laid the foundation for man's salvation in His precious atoning death on Calvary; that is a finished work. But during His life on earth

He began the work and ministry of preaching the gospel (see Hebrews 2:3-4), and this work He left *un*finished; He began to do it, as our text says.

Many have said that this book should not be called "the Acts of the Apostles," but rather "the acts of the Holy Spirit." The Spirit of God—guiding, empowering, indwelling, etc.—is seen often in this book. Without Him all human effort would be fruitless indeed. On the other hand, we must not forget that the Spirit uses you and me as His instruments, creating in our hearts the desire to serve the Lord and furnishing the power to do so (Philippians 2:13).

Let us for a moment, ere we begin our study of Acts, consider this "finished work of our Lord." What did Christ come to do?

First of all, He came to settle the great question of sin. God rested after He had made Heaven and earth, but soon His rest was disturbed by the fall of our parents in the garden of Eden. God's rest was broken in upon and He began to work again, as Jesus says in John 5:17. In due time Jesus came to earth to do the Father's will, and that will was that He might offer Himself a sacrifice for our sins (Hebrews 10:9-10). Sin merits divine judgment and the Lord Jesus died on the Cross under the weight of our guilt, bearing our judgment. Only He could do that work and, praise His Name, He did it. That is therefore a finished work, nevermore to be repeated.

Secondly, in His death the basis was laid to put away sin forever (Hebrews 9:26). Not only are the sins of a believer in Jesus blotted out forever, but sin itself shall be completely done away with; someday sin and its awful consequences shall disappear forever. Only in hell will there be any sinners left, and even they won't be permitted to sin any more, for all rebellion against God shall be subdued: every knee shall bow and every tongue confess Jesus Christ as Lord, to the glory of God the Father.

The work of the Cross Christ alone could do—and did. But He left a work unfinished; He left it for us to carry on: the work of preaching the gospel, and thus as the Spirit saves souls, seeing them built on the foundation laid at Calvary; seeing them added to the Church, which is the Body of Christ, composed of all true believers in Jesus. Every believer has the privilege as well as the responsibility of investing his time, talents, and tithes in that fruitful enterprise.

This unfinished work, which Jesus only *began* to do, is a great work. The Lord assured His disciples—in John 14: 12—that they were to do "greater" works than His, after He had gone back to the Father. Not greater in importance, of course, for nothing can compare with the infinite worth of the Cross, but greater in size and volume, even as the superstructure of a building is much larger than the foundation, though not as important. When Jesus went away He set the porter (typifying the Holy Spirit) to watch and gave to every man his work (Mark 13:34). Are you doing your share?

Remember these vital truths:

1. The Lord can use *you*. Every member in the Body of Christ has a special function to perform.

2. God can use you just as you are. We do not all have the same capacity, but He gives talents according to each man's individual ability.

3. Your usefulness will grow as you use what little you may have now. No one ever becomes a carpenter by wishing to be one or by watching another do carpentry, but only by doing the work himself. You may be hesitant and blundering at first, perhaps, but you will increase in ability by doing.

4. God will use you where you are. John 15:16 says He ordains those whom He chooses as His own. That word *ordain* is the simple word *put*. As the gardener puts the plants where he believes they will do best, so the Lord puts you and me to bear fruit for Him.

5. He will supply every need, and will reward you well when payday comes, at the Judgment Seat of Christ.

Jesus began to do and teach. Notice that the Lord *did* first; then taught. How unlike the Pharisees, who, as Jesus said, "say and do not." Let us not be Pharisees. The Lord always practised first, before He preached. He told the rich young ruler to sell all he had and to give to the poor; He Himself had done that very thing: He for our sakes became poor that we through His poverty might be rich. When He told the disciples to pray, "Thy will be done on earth," He added emphasis to that petition by Himself living a life wholly devoted to the Father's will (John 6:38). The Lord taught by example as much as by precept, and example is far more potent than precept. A holy life adds tremendous force to the mes-

sage we preach. Alas, how sadly the Church has failed
there. May God help each of us to do and be before we
tell others what to be and do!

After this brief reference—in the opening verse of
Acts—to his Gospel, Luke speaks of the forty days our
Lord spent with His disciples consequent to His resurrection, until He was taken up. They saw the Lord on a
number of occasions, on one of which He told them to
stay in Jerusalem until they should be baptized with the
Holy Spirit. Luke 24:49 records the actual statement.
The Lord reminds them of the words of John the Baptist, who said that Jesus would come and baptize with
the Holy Ghost (Matthew 3:11). In Acts 1:5 the Lord
tells His disciples that that day is now close at hand, "not
many days hence."

Verse 6 indicates that the apostles still did not understand the purpose of God. They were still thinking of a
literal kingdom here on earth, with Christ as Israel's
King. They still did not seem to realize that Israel had
definitely and finally rejected their Messiah; that God's
purpose was to gather out of the world a people for His
name: of Jew and Gentile through faith in a crucified
Christ, to form a new Body on earth—the Church. The
Lord does not reply directly to their question, because
not till the Holy Spirit came would they be fitted to understand fully God's Word, but He speaks of the empowering of the Spirit they were to receive in a few days.
He would fit them to be Christ's witnesses, as such beginning their ministry at Jerusalem, and gradually reaching
out to the utmost bounds of the earth. The book of Acts

unfolds this apostolic ministry. Slowly they would be delivered from their Judaistic prejudices and would learn that Israel as a nation was set aside and that the Cross of Christ was to be the means to unite Jew and Gentile into one Body.

"Taken Up"

ACTS 1:2,9,11,22

FOUR TIMES we read of the Lord Jesus being *taken up*. Luke 24:51 says He was "carried up into heaven." The suggestion is that a mighty host of angels accompanied our risen Lord into Heaven, where the everlasting doors were thrown open, and the King of glory entered in (Psalm 24), after having accomplished the mighty work of redemption at Calvary. Psalm 68:17 connects an honor guard of angels with the triumphant ascension of the Victorious Conqueror, after the victory won upon the Cross. We read there that the chariots of God are twenty thousands of angels . . . and then it goes on to say: "Thou hast ascended on high, Thou hast led captivity captive," a passage which Ephesians 4:8 connects directly with Christ's ascension. These thousands of angels are called the "chariots of God," and since angels are called "flaming fire" (Psalm 104:4), these chariots were thus chariots of fire—the very term used when Elijah was escorted to glory (2 Kings 2:11). The chariot in his case was nothing less than a host of angelic attendants. Even a believer's spirit seems to get a heavenly escort, as Lazarus was carried by angels into Abraham's bosom. Ere mourning relatives carry the body of a believer to the cemetery, a vast procession of angels has carried his soul and spirit to glory in a wonderful, though invisible to us, welcome.

The Ascension of the Lord Jesus Christ—what a glorious event it is! God set Him at His own right hand in the heavenlies, far above all principalities and power and might and dominion and every name that is named, not only in this world, but in that which is to come. "He hath put all things under His feet, and gave Him to be the head over all things to the Church, which is His Body, the fulness of Him that filleth all in all." This fourfold repetition of being "taken up" in this chapter is to remind us that we as believers are not only to know and to preach Christ as the One crucified, but also as the glorified One. The Church's true message is that the Son of God glorified is, from the glory, calling men to the obtaining of the glory (2 Thessalonians 2:14); that the Church is a heavenly Body with its Head in Heaven, and all its purposes, aims, and ambitions are heavenly.

1. We read that Jesus did and taught until the day He was taken up. He was ever the faithful and true witness, till the very end, setting us an example to imitate. We must not fail to live and preach Christ.

2. He was taken up and a cloud received Him out of

their sight. Henceforth His disciples were to walk entirely by faith. While on earth with their Lord, they had largely let Him do everything, as was proper. But now He is leaving them; and by the power of the Spirit which they were to receive on the day of Pentecost, they were now to go forth entirely dependent upon God. Though absent in body, the Lord would be with them in spirit, as He had assured them in Matthew 28:20, "Lo, I am with you always." From here on they were to practise what Paul urged on the Philippians: "But now much more in my absence, work out your own salvation with fear and trembling." The Christian path is one entirely of faith now, as then it was with them, for Jesus was taken up out of their *sight*. The Word of God is to be our authority and guide in everything.

3. "This same Jesus, which is taken up from you into heaven, shall so come in like manner as ye have seen Him go into heaven"—verse 11. Christ ascended from the Mount of Olives and when He returns to earth to reign shall come back to the very same place in the very same way (Zechariah 14:4).

4. "Beginning from the baptism of John, unto that same day that He was taken up from us, must one be ordained to be a witness with us of His resurrection"—verse 22. Yes, Jesus was taken up. He returned to glory—to the Father—but still His thoughts and eyes are here, watching over His ransomed people, to His gracious heart so dear. He encourages them, in these four passages: by His own example; by the impartation of the Holy Spirit, who would be with them to take the place

of their absent Lord; by the assurance that He would come back some day; and by making His disciples His competent witnesses during His absence.

After the Lord had gone to Heaven, the disciples went to Jerusalem and into an upper room, where they continued in prayer for the ten days between the Ascension of Christ and the descent of the Holy Spirit on the day of Pentecost. Three interesting subjects out of this first chapter—the infallible proofs of verse 3, the upper room of verse 13, and the "field of blood"—will be considered more at length under the list of special subjects at the end of this volume.

The Choosing of Matthias, in the Place of Judas

ACTS 1:15-26

JUDAS COMMITTED SUICIDE—sad betrayer of the Lord of glory. Peter quotes from Psalm 109:8 to show that another was to take Judas' place among the twelve (Acts 1:20). Peter speaks with such absolute conviction and assurance that it seems to me unwise to question that he was being guided by the Holy Spirit.

Various points are sometimes raised to suggest Peter and those with him made a mistake and that they should have waited till after the Holy Spirit had come; that Paul was intended to take Judas' place and fill out the complete number of the twelve. Why, say some, did they choose two men and cast lots upon them; why just two instead of a hundred or more? I believe the answer to that is that there were only two qualified to take a place with the twelve. Undoubtedly there were very few who walked with the Lord all during the three and a half years of His ministry, for Peter says they must have been with them without a break during that period. We read on one occasion that many of His disciples went back and walked no more with Him. It is not likely that there were many who continued all the time; I suggest there were only two who met the qualifications.

As to the casting of lots, the rightness of which is also occasionally questioned, this was a familiar Old Testament way of deciding important issues, used not only by men, but upon the order and under the guidance of Jehovah Himself, as for instance in the dividing of the land to the twelve tribes. Proverbs 16:33 shows that "the lot is cast into the lap; but the whole disposing thereof is of the Lord." That the Apostle Paul was meant to be of the twelve and have the place given here to Matthias is, I believe, untenable in the general light of Scripture, for the following reasons:

1. Paul himself in nowise ever hints that he should have been one of the twelve. In fact, he rather hints that he felt unworthy to be an apostle at all, because he persecuted the Church of God (1 Corinthians 15:9).

2. Again and again—in the earlier chapters of Acts, before Saul's conversion—the apostles are mentioned as

under the Holy Spirit's inspiration (2:42-43; 4:33; 5:12; 6:6; etc., etc.), never with the intimation that all the twelve were not recognized as such by God. In fact, in Acts 6:2 we read that "the twelve" called the multitude of the disciples unto them. Here the Holy Spirit definitely recognizes Matthias as one of the *twelve*. This is the more striking when we know that after the defection of Judas, the apostles were known *not* as the twelve, but as the *eleven* (see Matthew 28:16; Mark 16:14; Luke 24:9, 33). That they are now called the twelve, after Judas has been replaced by Matthias, is a clear proof, in my judgment, that the action of the disciples in the upper room, when they chose Matthias, is justified as divinely correct.

Incidentally, it is interesting to note that John 20:24 is an exception to Matthew, Mark, and Luke. Though Judas was no longer with the disciples, John still calls them the "twelve," whereas all the others speak of them as "the eleven." I believe there is a remarkable, solemn thought here. Thomas was absent that resurrection day, and so was Judas; his absence put him, to all outward appearances, in Judas' class. That's why we read he was one of the twelve, thus still including Judas among the disciples. It could not be said that Thomas was one of the eleven on this occasion, though actually he was, for by his absence he took the same place as Judas. The eleven were the Lord's faithful followers, and that night Thomas was not faithful, for he was absent.

We read again in Acts 2:14 that Peter stood up with the eleven, himself of course being the twelfth. Here again the pen of Holy Writ acknowledges Matthias as one of the twelve. I believe it is a mistake to think Paul should have been one of the twelve, for:

Paul was the apostle to the uncircumcision, while the others' special mission was to the circumcision. The twelve were apostles because they had been saved by Christ on earth, and were to be witnesses of His wondrous life and death.

Paul was saved by a Christ who had left the earth, and who reached this sinner from the glory, and so Paul was to be a witness of Christ in glory.

The twelve had seen Christ on earth, which was a requisite to apostleship. Paul had not, but had seen Christ in glory (1 Corinthians 9:1), which he tells us entitled him to be an apostle; but for that very reason an apostle in another way than were the twelve.

They had been won to Christ during the time of His humiliation; Paul after the hour of his exaltation.

These considerations and others put Paul into an entirely different category from the twelve apostles. Their ministry largely has to do with Christ as Saviour, the value of His death, and the believer's life on earth, as he is traveling on to Heaven (1 Peter 1:1-4). Paul's ministry, in sharp contrast, sets before the believer a Christ in glory, with all our blessings in heavenly places and our inheritance already enjoyed by the ministry of the Spirit, who is the firstfruits of all that someday we shall enjoy by sight. As the two ministries are different, so the two apostleships are separate.

2

The Baptism of the Spirit

"AND WHEN the day of Pentecost was fully come, they were all with one accord in one place. And suddenly there came a sound from heaven as of a rushing mighty wind, and it filled all the house where they were sitting. And there appeared unto them cloven tongues like as of fire, and it sat upon each of them.

"And they were all filled with the Holy Ghost, and began to speak with other tongues, as the Spirit gave them utterance"—Acts 2:1-4

It is said of John the Baptist, in each of the Gospels, that he baptized with water, but that the Lord was to baptize with the Holy Ghost and with fire. The Lord refers to this in Acts 1:5, saying the disciples were to be baptized with the Holy Ghost not many days hence. This shows that the descent of the Holy Spirit on Pentecost is spoken of as the "baptism" of the Spirit, for it was to take place, as Jesus said "not many days hence." The tremendous event of the coming of the Holy Spirit to abide in this world as He dwells in His Church, is therefore called the baptism of the Spirit. Since the Spirit came on this occasion, and has been here ever since (John 14:16), and this coming is called His baptism, we come to the conclusion there is only *one* baptism of the Spirit given in Scripture. Many speak today about a baptism of the Spirit, but I do not think the Bible supports this thought. Not once after Pentecost, to which Acts 1:5 has reference, is the term "baptizing with the Spirit" found in Scripture. Peter says—in Acts 11:16—that the event in Cornelius' home reminded him of what the Lord had said in Acts 1:5; but when the actual conversion of Cornelius took place and the Holy Ghost came upon those Gentile converts, the term *baptize* is not used; it is said that the Holy Ghost fell on them. On no occasion, either of those in Acts 8, or of the Ethiopian eunuch in the same chapter, or of Cornelius in chapter 10, or of those believers in Acts 19:6 is the word *baptize* used.

The only occasion is in 1 Corinthians 12:13, where we are told that "by one Spirit are we all baptized into one body." This, in connection with the subject of that chapter, has in view the very thing that happened on the day of Pentecost—the formation of the Church as the Body of Christ by the baptism of the Spirit. The text in 1 Corinthians 12:13 is very exact. It does not say by one Spirit is *each one* baptized into *the* Body, as though it refers to the operation of the Holy Spirit at each individual's conversion, but "are we *all* baptized." It is a united action—the forming of till-then-individual believers into the mystical body of Christ—the Church. Nor does it say that each is baptized into *the* body, but all into *one* body. The oneness—the unity of the saints—is in view in this baptism.

I believe in every case, unless stated to be the baptism of the *Spirit*, baptism in the New Testament has in view the baptism in water.

When the tabernacle was dedicated to its service in Israel, the "glory of the Lord" filled it (Exodus 40:35) and when the temple of the Lord was set apart, again the glory of the Lord filled the house of the Lord (1 Kings 8:11). These two buildings were Old Testament types of the Church as God's spiritual house. So, as the Church, the house of God built of living stones, is about to be ordained to be God's witness upon the earth, again the glory of the Lord fills it (Acts 2:2). The Holy Spirit, under the simile of a mighty wind, fills all the house.

The number three is prominent at this great event, perhaps to suggest the interest of the triune Godhead—the Father who gave His Son, the Son who gave Himself, and the Spirit who is to make all this good to us and through us.

1. The Spirit did three things: He filled the house (verse 2); He came *upon* each believer (verse 3); He came *into* each of them to abide (verse 4), for they were all filled with the Holy Ghost. He filled all the house, because the Church corporately is the "temple of the living God" (1 Corinthians 3:16). He came upon each believer, to furnish power for Christian life and testimony. The disciples were to be "endued with power from on high" (Luke 24:49). He filled each believer with Himself, for the indwelling Spirit has precious threefold ministry: for, in, and through the believer. He seals each for security; He gives the earnest—the foretaste of eternal blessings—for satisfaction; and He anoints for service.

2. In connection with the Scriptures, the Holy Spirit

furnishes: inspiration (2 Peter 1:21); revelation (1 Corinthians 2:10); illumination (1 Corinthians 2:13).

3. As to the *past*, as a teacher, He brings all things to remembrance (John 14:26); as to the *present*, He takes the things of Christ and shows them unto us (John 16:14-15); as to the *future*, He will show us things to come (John 16:13).

4. As to the world, He convicts it of sin, of righteousness, and of judgment (John 16:8-11).

The Spirit was accompanied by three phenomena: He came as a rushing, mighty *wind*, as tongues of *fire*, and as *tongues*. He made Himself felt, seen, and heard. In these three we have suggestions as to the Spirit's ministry in regeneration, sanctification, and proclamation.

Wind. In John 3, the wind is employed as a type of the Spirit in the work of new birth. The Greek word for spirit is the same as that for wind. As the wind does not always blow with the same intensity, so the Spirit of God operates in various ways. No two people are saved alike, or have the same spiritual experience. Some are won to Christ as it were by the sweet gentle breeze of His love drawing them; others are shaken as by a fearful gale of conviction and fear. The wind does not always blow with hurricane force, so the Spirit does not convict every soul after the same manner. But in the case of every conversion, it is the Spirit's operation that is felt, even as the wind is felt, though not seen by us.

Fire. Fire is often used in the Bible in connection with sanctification or purification. Isaiah 4:4 speaks of cleansing by the spirit of judgment and the spirit of burning. In Isaiah 6:7 a coal of fire took away Isaiah's iniquity, and set his lips afire for God. "While I mused," says David, "the fire burned and I spake with my tongue" (Psalm 39:3). Fire set the incense aglow, and the fire of the Spirit burning in our hearts will set them on fire— aglow with zeal and devotion to Him. Here we have sanctification by the Spirit, as regeneration in the first case.

Tongues. With those tongues touched by the Spirit, they began to speak, preaching the gospel to the multitudes gathered there. To us too has been committed the ministry of reconciliation. Sometimes we sing: "Oh for a thousand tongues to sing." May God help us to use the one we have! God confounded the languages at the tower of Babel; here by the Spirit He spoke to many thousands each in their own tongue to reach them with the story of redeeming love.

Peter explains to the crowd that this mighty event is a partial fulfillment of Joel's prophecy. It was only partial, for in the future day of which Joel prophesied, the Spirit was to be poured out upon "all" flesh, and this certainly did not take place at Pentecost. It was a foreshadowing of Israel's future conversion to God as a nation; a conversion then, and till today, still hindered by the nation's continued rejection of her Saviour and Lord. Peter goes on to charge the nation with that terrible sin and to offer, to those who would repent, remission of sins and the impartation of the Holy Ghost (verse 38).

"Be This Known Unto You"

ACTS 2:14

WITH THESE WORDS Peter opens his great sermon. Read this powerful message in verses 14 to 40. It has been said that Peter gives:

1. An explanation concerning "this"—verse 12.
2. A proclamation concerning "Him"—verses 22-36.
3. An application concerning "them"—verses 37-40.

As to the first, some said the apostles were drunk. No, says Peter, not as ye suppose are these drunk (which is the sense of the passage, so I understand). They were drunk after a fashion, but not with wine, wherein is excess; but they were filled with the Spirit (Ephesians 5:18). Wine gives an artificial exhilaration; the Spirit an holy elevation. Wine stimulates evil; the Holy Spirit incites toward good. Man has that let-down feeling after the stimulation of wine recedes, but the Holy Spirit builds spiritual strength and stability of character. Men filled with wine often act foolishly; those filled with the Spirit speak forth the Word of God in truth and soberness.

Filled with the Spirit, Peter and the others spoke (verse 4). This is very noticeable, in the book of Acts as well as elsewhere in Scripture, as in Acts 2:4; 4:8; 4:31; 9:17,20; etc. In each of these cases being full of the Spirit is followed by "speaking." One of the true marks of a Spirit-filled saint is that he speaks.

Peter tells his audience that this phenomenon of men speaking the works of God was not something entirely unexpected, for it had been foretold by the prophet Joel. The Spirit was to be poured out upon all flesh; even servants and handmaidens were to prophesy. The simplest believer, by the enablement of the Spirit of God, would now be able to tell forth the grace and glory of God. This that took place at Pentecost was only a partial fulfillment of Joel's prophecy, for the signs in Heaven above and earth beneath look on to Christ's future Coming in judgment; when the nation of Israel shall be converted, then the Spirit shall be poured out on "all" flesh.

As to the second point, Peter's sermon here, as well as those in chapters 3, 4, and 5, strongly stresses Israel's sin in the rejection and crucifixion of their Messiah, and on the other hand God's love in making that very crime on their part the basis for salvation. He proves his contentions by quotations from the Old Testament and winds up his charge by telling them that God has made "that same Jesus, whom ye have crucified, both Lord and Christ."

It has been noted by many the strong emphasis there is in these chapters on the Resurrection of the Lord Jesus. It is mentioned in these sermons about twice as often as is His death. As we read in Acts 4:33: "With great power gave the apostles witness of the resurrection of the Lord Jesus." Thousands upon thousands saw the death of Christ, for there were vast crowds in Jerusalem when our blessed Lord hung upon the cross; but not one eye saw Him rise from the dead, or saw Him after His resurrection, except His disciples only (see Acts 10:41). Therefore His resurrection needed far more emphasis, since it had to be taken entirely by faith. Again, His death was not unusual (from the outward aspect), for all men die; but His resurrection was not human in any way, but absolutely divine. None but He alone ever rose by his own power from the dead. Therefore, to believe in the Resurrection of Christ is tantamount to confessing His deity. Confessing His deity in view of His resurrection is at the same time to confess the atoning value of His death; for if His resurrection proves He is God, then His death could not have been the death of a sinner, but of a Saviour. Hence, I believe, the Resurrection of our Saviour was so emphatically declared and still should be, for "if thou shalt confess with thy mouth the Lord Jesus, and shalt believe in thine heart that God hath raised Him from the dead, thou shalt be saved."

In the third place, they were pricked in their heart. Peter once used the sword in the wrong way because he used the wrong sword. When he chopped off Malchus' ear, then Peter slashed a piece off on the outside. Here he used the sword *of the Spirit* and used it rightly to reach the inside. The Word of God is a sharp two-edged sword —with which to stab, not slash. Sometimes preachers use the Scriptures to slash and smash and all they succeed in doing is to chop off pieces on the outside; they make big wounds with little results. The aim of God's Word is to reach the inside—the conscience and the heart. Thus the sword makes the smallest wounds but accomplishes the greatest and most permanent results.

"What shall we do?" cried many. "Repent, and be baptized," said Peter, "in the name of Jesus Christ for the remission of sins, and ye shall receive the gift of the Holy Ghost."

Baptism

ACTS 2:38

THE WORD OF GOD does not teach that one cannot be saved unless he is baptized. In fact, it teaches the opposite. In verse 41 of Acts 2 it states that they who gladly received His Word were baptized; certainly those who gladly received the Word of God were believers and therefore, as believers, they were baptized. The same holds true in Acts 8:12, where the Samaritans believed and were baptized. Even more pronounced is this thought in Acts 10. Cornelius and his friends had already received the Holy Ghost before Peter ordered their baptism. Yea, Peter said: "Can any man forbid water, that these should not be baptized, *which have received the Holy Ghost* as well as we?" This in clear terms tells us that if they had not received the Holy Ghost, they would have been ineligible for baptism; thus baptism followed their conversion—they were saved before they were baptized. The same order is found in Acts 18:8, where the Corinthians heard, believed, and then were baptized.

Acts 22:16 is sometimes cited as a proof that in baptism one's sins are forgiven, but it is difficult to see how any true believer can make such a contention in the light of the Scripture which says that it is the *blood* of Jesus Christ that cleanseth from *all* sin. The explanation of Acts 22:16 is of course that Paul there was told to wash away his sins himself. He was told to do it. Does a sinner wash away his own guilt before God? Certainly not. Then baptism in water is simply the believer's act in washing away his sins in the sight of men. Washing is an external act, not internal. By being baptized a believer says, as it were, that he is through with his sin.

The same truth is presented in other ways to believers who already are in Christ, for if any man is in Christ he is a new creature (2 Corinthians 5:17). Yet to such Pauí says, "Put ye on the Lord Jesus Christ" (Romans 13:14); in other words—get *in* Christ, for that is what you do when you put *on* something. To those who already are in Christ Paul says to get in Christ. What is the explanation? The explanation is that, by our faith in Christ as Saviour, God places us in His Son; by our daily living for Him, the world sees us in Christ. The one is our position before God; the other our position before men. This is the very thought in connection with baptism as in Galatians 3:27: "As many as have been baptized into Christ have put on Christ." By faith we are in Christ before God; by baptism we are in Christ before men; it is our confession where they can see and know it, proving that we are Christians.

In our text in Acts 2:38, Peter is not implying that by being baptized they would receive remission of their sins. The word "for" is "unto." It simply states that their repentance would lead to the remission of their sins: it would be "unto" remission of sins; and this is still just as true today. We have already seen that their baptism followed upon their faith (verse 41). Their baptism showed the reality of their repentance. The same is true of those passages in Mark 1:4 and Luke 3:3, where it is said that John preached the baptism of repentance for [unto] the forgiveness of sins. There was no salvation at all in that baptism, for John himself said he only baptized with water, but He that is to "come after me . . . He shall baptize you with the Holy Ghost." So does Acts 19:5 prove that John's baptism was not Christian baptism at all, for otherwise Paul would not have baptized those disciples of John again—this time in the Name of Jesus.

A Scripture used by advocates of conversion by baptism is 1 Peter 3:20-21: "Which sometime were disobedient, when once the longsuffering of God waited in the days of Noah, while the ark was a preparing, wherein few, that is, eight souls were saved by water. The like figure whereunto even baptism doth also now save us . . . by the resurrection of Jesus Christ." The contention is that Noah's and his family's salvation in the ark illustrates how today people are saved by baptism.

I once asked a Mormon elder, who advanced this idea,

if he would please tell me who were baptized in Noah's day—the saved or the lost? Not a drop of water touched Noah and his family; all those who went into the water of baptism were drowned. It puzzled him a bit and he replied, "Then, what does it mean when it says they were saved by water?" The answer is that it means just what it says. They were saved by water, but not the water that fell on them, for none fell on them. They were saved by the water that fell on the ark. The waters burst from beneath (typical of man's hatred and wickedness that nailed the Son of God to the cross), and the waters came from above (typical of the judgment from above which our blessed Saviour bore on the cross). Yes, those waters typify the waves and billows of judgment which lifted Christ—our Ark of safety—up on the cross. It is by that redemptive work that we are saved. Those waters of judgment fell on Him; not on us. Like Noah and his family we who are believers are safe and secure in Christ. We are saved by the baptism of judgment Christ knew at Calvary; not by the baptism of water. The text in 1 Peter does not say that we are saved by baptism. It says that baptism is a "like" figure. Both Noah's ark and baptism prefigure the same thing; they picture the work of Christ as He bore our sins and rose victoriously from the dead.

There is a progression of truth in regard to baptism in the book of Acts. In Acts 2, where the message is directed to the Jews who had crucified Christ, the command is "repent, be baptized, ye shall receive the Holy Spirit."

Their repentance of the act of crucifying their Messiah was to show the genuineness of their conversion and be proven by their baptism.

In Acts 8, where the gospel goes forth to the Samaritans, the "repent" is left out; they believed the message concerning the Name of Jesus Christ. Then they were baptized and received the Spirit. In Acts 10, with the gospel this time preached to Gentiles, there is the preaching of the Word, followed by faith, and this in turn by the impartation of the Holy Spirit, and then baptism because they were believers. And this latter order is consistently followed in the rest of the Bible, for the gospel today goes out to all men alike. Baptism is simply a confession, on the part of the believer, of his faith in Christ. It has no saving virtue, but will have a sanctifying influence upon the heart and life of the believer who in this way has publicly taken a stand for Christ.

The Fellowship of Saints

ACTS 2:41-47

THREE THOUSAND were saved: a large number and yet— how few, when the whole nation should have turned to God. But it was a time of great rejoicing nevertheless. The Lord's prophecy in John 10, that He as the good

Shepherd would lead His own sheep out from the sheep-fold, was now being carried out, for in this new society called the Church only those who believed came together (verse 44). One of the great blessings of Christianity is the fellowship of saints. In Judaism no provision was made for the gathering together of the people, except on special occasions as at the annual feasts. The Tabernacle and Temple were no meeting places for ministry or fellowship. But devout folk even then longed for get-to-gethers; eventually synagogues were built, of which we read so much in the four Gospels and in the book of Acts. Their origin is obscure. Some scholars claim their impetus came at the time of the Babylonian exile and that they were continued ever since. The urge to come together could not be so strong then as it is now, for in Judaism believers and unbelievers were all together and there can be no real fellowship between them. But, oh what a privilege it is to meet with others of like mind and to do what these early believers did, as recorded in verse 42: "They continued stedfastly in the apostles' doctrine and fellowship, and in breaking of bread, and in prayers." In this fourfold purpose for coming together we recognize the four different kinds of meetings prominent among us to this day:

1. The teaching or preaching of the Word of God. We have the apostles' doctrine in the written New Testament Scriptures. Teaching is mentioned first, for a knowledge of God and of His ways is vital to intelligent, vibrant Christian life and testimony.

2. Fellowship with saints. Believers should meet to-

gether, in separation from the world. There is nothing for the soul of the saint in this sinful world. One feels like a stranger in it, but oh! how good it is to get "home" among one's own brothers and sisters in Christ.

3. Breaking of bread. Some say this verse does not allude to the Lord's supper, but it would hardly seem necessary to state that these Christians kept on eating their daily meals. I believe we see here how those early believers honored our Lord's last request to remember Him in the breaking of the bread and partaking of the cup. How fresh and sweet the Saviour's last words would be to them. May they be so to us, too!

4. In prayers.

So in these four we have the ministry meeting; that for fellowship and social intercourse; our worship service when we come together to remember Him "until He come"; and last, but not least, the meeting for united prayer. They continued stedfastly in those; may we do the same. Let us not forsake the assembling of ourselves together, as the manner of some is!

Those were the bright, happy days of first love. Too bad that nothing lasts very long when man has something to do with it. Oh, that we may value more those inexpressibly precious privileges; yet how many neglect them sadly.

3

The Lame Man Healed

ACTS 3:1-16

THE LAME BEGGAR, lying at the gate of the temple, is, I believe, a picture of the nation of Israel. This man's condition reminds one of a similar one in John 5, where the Lord Jesus Himself performed the miracle of restoring that one, who had been afflicted thirty-eight years. Those thirty-eight years are reminiscent of the thirty-eight years Israel wandered in the wilderness, illustrating how Israel was unable spiritually to walk to the glory of God. This man is near the Holy Place yet so far from it, for he is unable to enter. So Israel, instead of entering to present their gifts to God, are outside, scattered throughout the world, begging alms from men. They were under the law, which they broke (as did all of us); a law called in Galatians 4:9 the "weak and beggarly elements." Weak because man is without strength to do God's will; beggarly because, like with this lame man, it leaves the sinner a beggar. It is only the free grace of God that can bestow true riches and can change the beggar into a millionaire, blessed with the unsearchable riches of Christ. Israel is seen here (typified by this beggar) outside the temple, for as a nation they were away from God. But Jesus Himself was outside too, for in

Matthew 23:38 He said that their house was left unto them desolate. Rejected by Israel, He too was on the outside. And by the power of the Name of the rejected Saviour this man is made whole. For beggarly sinners outside an empty temple there is hope in the very Saviour they refused. He is on the outside too. An empty religion leaves men beggars. But praise God, there is hope in the Name—and only in His Name—of Jesus!

This lame man was laid at the gate of the temple which is called Beautiful. I understand that this gate, furnished by Herod, was made of precious Corinthian brass—80 feet high and 65 feet broad. It took about twenty men to close it. But we know of a gate more beautiful—a gate Israel did not recognize—a door into the very presence of God, for Jesus is the Door. Only through Him is there entrance into the holiest of all.

Lying there daily, helpless, this man might well have begun to think that God's blessing was only for those who were whole, not for the sick or deformed. He could not enter, no matter how much he wished to do so. The law likewise has a message only for the strong; only the righteous need apply. But God's grace is offered to all —to the sick and helpless, the weary and heavy-laden.

Peter and John came at the ninth hour—the hour of prayer. This was the hour when the daily burnt offering was offered upon the altar; the very hour our blessed Lord died. It was the hour when the incense was burned upon the golden altar, speaking of Christ in His perfection. It was in view of the value of the death and worth of Christ that blessing came to this poor beggar.

"Silver and gold have I none," said Peter. If that is what you are looking for, do not look to Christ. He does not promise to those who believe on Him material gain. Usually it is the poor who listen to the gospel. Faith in Christ does not make them rich with earth's goods, but makes them rich in faith and heirs of the coming kingdom. Money has great value in many ways but it cannot atone for sin, ease sorrow, or relieve suffering. It can buy a fancy tombstone, but it cannot take the sting out of death or cancel divine judgment.

Peter had no money, yet he could impart a blessing all the money on earth cannot buy. Like Paul, so Peter—and any believer—can make many rich, though poor in earthly goods. It is great to be God's messenger, with the right to dispense wealth that goes beyond all human calculations. Peter brought this cripple great riches, without becoming poorer in doing so. God's grace too is for all, yet makes Him no poorer. In fact, the more we give away of God's bounty, the greater our store of it becomes.

Peter took him by the right hand and lifted him up. This suggests that the beggar held out his hand too, so that Peter might grasp it. That is how God's saving grace is imparted. Hands are used for receiving as well as for giving. God's big hand is full of love and grace; all the sinner needs to do is hold out his little hand and receive. And, after we have received from Him, how pleasant it is to give now to others.

The healed man not only walked, but leaped, and entered with them into the temple, praising God. Not only was he healed physically, but his soul had come to rejoice in the Lord; he was healed body and soul.

First Peter held him by the hand (verse 7); then the beggar held Peter (verse 11). They continued holding hands. The beggar did not hold Peter and John for the sake of support, for he leaped; he did not need to hold them for that reason. No doubt he held the apostles' hands out of gratitude; in the joy of happy fellowship and identification with these newfound friends. So it is well, when one is saved, to cling in fellowship and to stand by the side of those who have brought us to Christ. Later we read (Acts 4:14) that when the Jewish leaders saw the man who was healed standing with the apostles, they could say nothing against it. Immediately his testimony for Christ counted.

What a difference now! Not a beggar on the outside, but rejoicing and praising God on the inside (verse 8). This drew crowds who were impressed by the miracle and Peter used the opportunity to preach the gospel to them.

The Name of Jesus

ACTS 3:16

THAT "NAME" is found thirty-three times in the book of Acts, far more than in any other book of the New

Testament. We find Him mentioned by that Name six times in chapter 4 in connection with the ministry of the apostle Peter, and six times in chapter 9 in connection with Paul.

How much there is in a name! Sometimes, when one is seeking a favor, a friend may direct you to someone else and say, "When you see him, mention my name." The use of a name may mean a good position for you; it may get you some special privilege; it may even reprieve a death sentence. But a human name has limits. It does not go beyond the human sphere. No name of any creature has any special weight with God. He honors fully only one name—the Name of Jesus. No creature is beyond the reach of that Name. All animate and even inanimate creation acknowledges the power of that Name.

Says Peter to the men of Israel: "His name through faith in His name hath made this man strong" (Acts 3:16). All blessing is found in that Name, and faith releases that power for our benefit. Even in this world one must have authorization to use another's name. Christ never gave His Name to sinners to use, unless first the sinner has believed on His Name, and thus has become a child of God (John 1:12). After that, there is untold blessing available for the believer in that Name of Jesus.

We are encouraged to ask what we will—in the Name of Jesus.

We have the assurance of His presence, when we meet in His Name.

We are to depart from iniquity when we name the Name of Christ.

In chapter 3 Peter declares the worth of the precious Name of Jesus, as he spoke to the common people. In chapter 4 he is brought before the impressive conclave of the Jewish leaders and when asked by what power or by what name he healed the lame man, he again declares that it is through "the name of Jesus Christ of Nazareth, whom ye crucified, whom God raised from the dead, even by Him doth this man stand here before you whole." And then, implying that this physical healing was but an illustration of God's way of saving a soul (as all such miracles in the Gospels and in Acts are), Peter passes from the physical to the spiritual aspect in saying—in verse 12—"Neither is there salvation in any other; for there is none other name under heaven given among men, whereby we must be saved." Look at this full declaration of the gospel in this text. There are at least three interesting things here:

1. There "*is*" salvation. Praise God, Peter did not have to say there "was" salvation. Neither could he say there "will be" salvation, for only God knows when the day of grace shall end, when it will be forever too late to be saved. Are *you* saved? Remember that today is the day of salvation; not tomorrow.

2. Salvation is not in any other. It is not in yourself, not in the priest or the preacher, not in the church, not in your parents. It is only and alone in Christ. Jesus alone can save.

3. It is in the Name of Jesus. Years ago a common catch phrase used to be, "What's in a name?" There may be so much in a name.

When I first began to devote my time to preach the Word in dependence on the Lord for support, someone sent me a check for $50—a big sum in those days. I presented it at a local bank, but they refused to give me the cash because they knew neither the signer of the check nor me. After a few days I found a Christian in that town, who kindly endorsed the check for me. He was a terrible scribbler, could not write nearly as well as I could, but after the teller took one look at that signature, he paid me the $50 without hesitation. There was $50 in that man's name for me. There is eternal life for every sinner in the Name of Jesus.

I imagine there are many who think that, when they stand before the throne of God, they will say to Him: "Don't you know me? I was a member of the church; I contributed of my money to religious work; I did this and that and the other." But God will look at them as the bank teller looked at me and will say, as it were: "I am sorry, but we never heard of you up here. The only name that counts here is the Name of Jesus. You should have His signature on your check. In His Name you may have everything; without His Name nothing." To all sinners at the judgment throne will come the verdict: "Depart, I never knew you."

This Name counts for salvation, as our text says, only *under Heaven*. As we read in Matthew 9:6, the Son of Man hath power *on earth* to forgive sins. There is no salvation once man has left this earth. God hath highly exalted Him and given Him a Name above every name. May you too honor this precious Name!

4

Witnesses of the Resurrection

ACTS 4:23-33

THERE ARE four major addresses by Simon Peter; one in each of chapters 2 to 5. Some are addressed to the common people, others to the leaders of the nation. Peter boldly witnesses for his Lord. While once he himself denied the Lord, now he charges the leaders with the same sin (Acts 3:14). He denied his Lord because of cowardice; they because of diabolical hatred and envy. But Peter bitterly repented of his grievous sin, and so he urges his hearers to repent too, and be baptized in the Name of Jesus. Such plain talk cut to the heart, and they took counsel to slay the apostles (Acts 5:33).

Peter and the others proved the promise of the Lord who said, "Ye shall receive power, after that the Holy Ghost is come upon you: and ye shall be witnesses unto Me." Peter tells them: "The God of our fathers raised up Jesus, whom ye slew and hanged on a tree. Him hath God exalted . . . to be a Prince and a Saviour, to give repentance to Israel, and forgiveness of sins. And we are His witnesses of these things. . . ." (Acts 5:30-32)

Special emphasis was laid by Peter upon the Resurrection of the Lord. It is mentioned some twelve times in the first five chapters; as in Acts 1:22; 2:32; 3:15; 4:2; 4:33; etc. The Resurrection of our Lord is of the most extremely vital importance. Without it His death would have been the most awful tragedy; without it we would still be in our sins (1 Corinthians 15:17). With it, His death proves to be indeed a mighty victory over all evil; the delivering power to everyone who believes in Jesus. For He was delivered for our offences and raised again for our justification.

His enemies had so hoped that by nailing Him to the cross, they would forever be rid of Him; but now they hear His Name more than ever before. As they say in Acts 5:28: "Ye have filled Jerusalem with your doctrine, and intend to bring this man's blood upon us." Ah, they were finding out that the Saviour's death was not the end, but rather the beginning of everything. He arose, as some day they shall be raised from the dead. Death— neither his own death nor the death of Christ—does not get the sinner out of trouble. But it does just that for the believer in Jesus. Christ's death puts away the believer's sin; and my death will be the gateway to the glory above.

"Ye intend to bring this man's blood upon us," said they. But they had done that themselves, as they stated before Pilate: "His blood be on us, and on our children" (Matthew 27:25). The blood of Christ is upon every soul—either for salvation or for damnation.

Listen to Peter's charge before the Sanhedrin in Acts

5:29-32: "We ought to obey God rather than men. The God of our fathers raised up Jesus, whom ye slew and hanged on a tree. Him hath God exalted with His right hand to be a Prince and a Saviour, for to give repentance to Israel, and forgiveness of sins. And we are His witnesses of these things; and so is also the Holy Ghost, whom God hath given to them that obey Him." Note Peter's God-consciousness. He speaks of God four times. When there is a clash between the commands of men and the command of God, no doubt can exist. We must obey God rather than man. How many have died for preaching Christ, when the authorities of earth forbade them to do so. Peter's strong words must have impressed at least one of his hearers. Gamaliel says: "If it be of God, ye cannot overthrow it, lest haply ye be found even to fight against God." God raised up Jesus; God hath highly exalted Him; God gives the Spirit to those who obey Him. It is important to be on God's side. There are three certainties in this passage of Scripture:

The certainty that God works (which we have just considered).

The certainty of Christ, expressed in the following three certainties:

(1) The assurance that He who died was raised from the dead by the Father. God's raising His Son sets His stamp of approval upon the infinite worth of the Saviour's death. (2) His exalted rank in the glory, for He ascended far above all principality and power. (3) The certainty of His mighty saving power, for He is the Sav-

iour, dispensing forgiveness of sins and rich blessing to every believer.

The certainty of the apostles' own calling. They were sent to bear witness to what they had seen and heard (Acts 4:20); and they would do so, even it meant suffering or martyrdom for His sake (Acts 5:41-42).

Being let go by the rulers, the servants of Christ went *to their own company* (Acts 4:23). In Acts 1:25 we read that Judas went "to his own place." How sad when hell is spoken of as one's "own" place. How much more precious when the saints are spoken of in Acts 4:23 as "their own" company. Freed by the authorities, these preachers just gravitated naturally to the gathering of the believers. Is that where *you* go when business or household duties set you free to go?

What a wonderful prayer meeting these believers had (verses 31-35). There was great quaking, followed by great power, with great grace upon them all.

We have not covered every verse (nor intend doing so) but have covered in general the truth set forth in the first five chapters. These are marked by the fiery preaching of the great facts of the Christian faith—the death and resurrection of Christ; by the response on the part of many who turned to Him in saving faith and gathered together to His Name alone; and by the corresponding opposition and persecution on the part of the unrepentant leaders.

5

Ananias and Sapphira

ACTS 5:1-11

THEY WERE bright, happy days of Christian love and fellowship—those early days of the Church's history. We read frequently of "gladness of heart, of praising God, of rejoicing." All that believed were together and had all things common. Many of them which heard the Word believed; multitudes were added to the Lord. And all this in spite of bitter persecution. The hatred of the world has never done the Church any harm; times of suffering have always been times of spiritual power. Persecution from without drives the sheep of the flock closer together, as happens when wolves attack the sheep. But once let the wolf get inside the flock and then he scatters the sheep. That is the sad story now related regarding Ananias and Sapphira.

The devil got inside. Corruption from within is far, far more dangerous than opposition from without. It is for this reason that God dealt with it so harshly; the Father judgeth every man's work (1 Peter 1:17).

We read in Acts 4:32 that all who believed were of one heart and one soul and that they had all things common. A brother named Barnabas (later Paul's fellow laborer) having land, sold it, brought the money, and laid it at the apostles' feet. Probably Barnabas' example led Ananias, with Sapphira his wife, to pretend equal devotion, thus perhaps hoping to gain influence and respect. But they gave only part of the money from the sale of a piece of property, while pretending to give it all. This would seem a small thing to be visited by such a severe penalty, wouldn't it? There are a number of possible replies to such a query:

1. It was the first seed of impurity sown in this glorious harvest of Pentecostal blessing. Real love was being displaced by hypocritical pretense; seed which has produced a horrible harvest all during the history of professing Christendom.

2. No sin is little. Witness the harvest of suffering this world has reaped from Eve's eating of one piece of fruit. There it was open disobedience; here it was pretended obedience.

3. Sin among the people of God is far more serious than among the unsaved. We believers are so well acquainted with the wonderful grace of God that we are apt to forget that sin in a Christian is no less heinous than in a sinner; in fact it is more so, for with the believer there is no excuse for it whatever. If God does not smite us dead today when we sin, as happened here to Ananias and Sapphira, it is not because it is less obnoxious in His sight, but only because in grace He tempers judgment now. Yet even today, according to 1 Corinthians 11:30, God will take believers out of the world by death if their lives are consistently dishonoring to Him. I have

no doubt this summary judgment was executed to tell saints that God does not condone sin in His people in any way.

4. God smote these two to indicate that morally the wages of sin is death. We have a sample of His judgment under grace, as there is also a sample under law, as seen in the case of the man who picked up sticks on the Sabbath day (Numbers 15:32-36). If God had continued that same severity of judgment, every Jew in the Old Testament would have been stoned to death, for none of them ever kept the law completely. If God today visited with death every Christian whose pretense is greater than his performance, not one of us would be alive. That judgment under law and this one under grace are samples, to remind us always that God hates sin—in us as much as in sinners—indeed, even more so. God hates sham. It is a healthy lesson to learn and ponder.

There seems to be almost a play upon a word in the name of this man Ananias, which means "the Lord has shown grace." Because the Lord has shown grace, this furnishes us with no excuse to prostitute that grace for selfish ends. Grace is no license for sinning, but should be the strongest possible incentive to holy living. The grace of God teaches us to deny ungodliness and worldly lusts, and to live soberly, righteously, and godly in this present world.

Some have questioned whether Ananias and Sapphira were real believers, but I am sure there can be no doubt as to that. Scripture clearly shows elsewhere that the

Lord does not judge sinners now, but He does judge His own people. Judgment must begin at the house of God (1 Peter 4:17). I Corinthians 11:31-32 teaches the same thing.

6

The Appointment of Deacons

ACTS 6: 1-7

ANOTHER EVIL arose, also within the Church. There was a murmuring of the Grecians against the Hebrews because their widows were neglected in the daily distribution—perhaps food or money. These Grecians were Jews as well as the others. There had always been a jealousy and rivalry between those Jews who had wandered to other countries and those who had stayed in the "old" country. Even true believers often are not immune to these nationalistic differences.

Hitherto the apostles themselves, in addition to their proper ministry of preaching Christ, had apparently attended to the physical needs of those among them. But they say that it was not right that they should leave the Word of God and serve tables. How many preachers need to realize that it is their business to preach Christ—not to serve on committees, or to raise money, or to engage in social welfare. There are others to attend to such things, which are important in their own place. But as the apostles said, "We will give ourselves continually to prayer, and to the ministry of the Word." They put prayer in the first place. Oh, how little time most of us take for prayer! And, if we are *continually* to minister the Word, we need much time for prayer, study, and meditation. How many messages lack for an evident paucity of thoughtful search of the Scriptures, and are dry because not watered abundantly by prayer. "It is needful to take time to be holy."

Let others tend to tables. That is the ministry of deacons, which simply means servants who lowly minister to the needs of God's people. Yet such too should be men of godly life, wise and gracious. Their qualifications are given in 1 Timothy 3:8-13. The congregation here chose them, but the apostles appointed them (verse 3). They were dedicated to their service by prayer and by the laying on of the hands of the apostles, who thus expressed their fellowship and approval of their service.

It is lovely to see that these seven men, chosen to look after the distribution of material things, were all Grecian Jews, as their names indicate. Since it is the Grecians that found fault, the saints reply by selecting men from their own group to serve as deacons. What a wonderfully gracious way to settle this incipient trouble! If the Grecians felt they could not trust their Hebrew brethren, they now learn that their brethren are ready to trust them. That is truly rewarding evil for good. What a joy if all differences among believers could be settled in such a humble, Christlike way!

We read in 1 Timothy 3:13 that they who "have used the office of a deacon well purchase to themselves a good degree, and great boldness in the faith which is in Christ Jesus." This is fully demonstrated here in Acts. At least two of these that we know of—Stephen and Philip—became outstanding ministers of the Word. One of these

—Stephen—spoke with such power that his enemies could not resist the spirit and wisdom by which he spoke. The other—Philip—was to go to Samaria and see great blessing as he preached Christ to the Samaritans.

Stephen, the First Christian Martyr

WE QUOTE here the closing seven verses of this wonderful seventh chapter of Acts, but urge the reading of the whole chapter through—a few times is better than just once. It is to me one of the most soul-stirring chapters in all the Word of God.

"When they heard these things, they were cut to the heart, and they gnashed on him with their teeth. But he, being full of the Holy Ghost, looked up stedfastly into heaven, and saw the glory of God, and Jesus standing on the right hand of God, And said, Behold, I see the heavens opened, and the Son of man standing on the right hand of God.

"Then they cried out with a loud voice, and stopped their ears, and ran upon him with one accord. And cast him out of the city, and stoned him: and the witnesses laid down their clothes at a young man's feet, whose name was Saul.

"And they stoned Stephen, calling upon God, and saying, Lord Jesus, receive my spirit. And he kneeled down, and cried with a loud voice, Lord, lay not this sin to their charge. And when he had said this, he fell asleep"—Acts 7:54-60

Stephen is not making an apology; he is not defending himself before this august council of Israel's religious leaders; nay, he is their judge, passing God's sentence on them. As another has said: "He is here the national conscience aroused by the power of the Spirit of God; he is the memory of the people, edged and sharpened; his is the voice of challenge and of conviction." Stephen's death at the close is but the re-enactment of the death of Christ; his judgment of the nation an echo of that pronounced at the Cross (John 12:31).

Stephen was a man full of faith and of the Holy Ghost, and is singled out from the other six in chapter 6. Full of faith and power he did great wonders and miracles among the people (verse 8). For the first time we hear of miracles being done by another than one of the apostles. Probably this special power was given to Stephen because he was about to face the whole nation, and his ability to do these great wonders would all the more add emphasis to his searching arraignment of the people; they would prove that he came empowered by divine credentials.

There is a striking similarity in some features connected with Stephen and those of our blessed Lord Himself. It impresses me that Stephen's martyr's death is meant to point the fact that his rejection is but the re-iterated rejection by the nation of Christ Himself. It is the exclamation mark to the period Israel set as to their destiny at Calvary. Jesus did miracles to prove who He was; Stephen did miracles to demonstrate that his mission was of God. Both were accused by false witnesses, with charges remarkably similar. Compare Acts 6:13-14 with Matthew 26:60-61.

Here in Acts 6:12 we read for the first time that the rulers and elders stirred up the common people, even as in Matthew 27:20 they persuaded the multitude to demand Christ's crucifixion.

They cast Stephen out of the city (Acts 7:58), even as our Saviour was led outside the city to be crucified.

Stephen prayed for his murderers (verse 60), even as the Lord on the cross prayed: "Father, forgive them; they know not what they do."

Stephen committed himself to the Lord as he prayed, "Lord Jesus, receive my spirit," as Christ said: "Father, into Thy hands I commend My Spirit."

Stephen in his dying moments cried with a "loud voice," as did our blessed Lord Himself (Matthew 27:50). These loud voices, are they not meant to tell the story that these deaths were not tragedies, but triumphs? They who said, "We do not want this man to reign over us," now had sent a messenger after Him, as our Lord had prophesied in Luke 19:14, confirming their unalterable refusal of God's Son.

In his address to the jury (the nation is the jury in this case), which pronounces the verdict of guilty on itself by slaying the prosecutor and stopping their ears to the sound of the accusing voice (verse 57), Stephen marshals the salient facts of Israel's history to prove that they ever rejected God's grace while failing to obey His law. Instead of judging themselves, they judged their deliverers and saviors, climaxing it with the murder of the Greatest Deliverer of all. Stephen quotes Abraham to prove that God's blessing was bestowed upon him entirely on the principle of faith. The very rite of circumcision was meant to illustrate the doing away with the flesh; Abraham got the blessing in Isaac when he himself was past age—when the flesh was dead.

Stephen cites samples of their persistent hatred of all that is good by reminding them of their sale of Joseph into Egypt because of envy; yet he became their savior. He goes very slowly over the story of Moses— taking more than twenty verses in our Bible for that purpose—to drive home to them the truth that he in whom they boasted was their chief accuser, as the Lord said in John 5:45. They utterly failed to recognize the self-sacrifing love that led Moses for their sakes to renounce the honors and emoluments of Egypt's throne, even as later a greater than Moses in matchless love laid aside His royal robes to become obedient unto death, even the death of the cross. Joseph they sold in envy; Moses they abused and refused. They put a full period to their sad wickedness and hatred by becoming the betrayers and the murderers of that "Just One."

Summing up his seething address, Stephen charges them with high treason against God the Father, the Son, and the Holy Spirit. Hebrews 10:29 tells us there is no remedy left for those who "insult" the Spirit of grace.

Stephen rebukes them not as the Israel of God, but as uncircumcised in heart and ears. Their final "no" to God in the martyrdom of Stephen has forfeited their title to be called any more God's chosen people; they are, as it were, only Gentiles in His sight—uncircumcised.

7

A Handful of Gems in Acts 7

VERSE 2. The God of glory appeared unto Abraham.
In Genesis 12:1 we read only that God spoke to Abraham; here we learn the additional fact that Abraham
also saw the Lord. Vision and voice operating together
converted Abraham from an idolator into a worshiper
of the true God, henceforth to walk by faith. Saul of
Tarsus was won in like manner.

Verse 22. Moses was mighty in words and deeds. We
would not know this from the record of the Old Testament. We learn here that Moses did not speak the truth
when he said to God: "O my Lord, I am not eloquent,
neither heretofore, nor since Thou hast spoken unto
Thy servant: but I am slow of speech, and of a slow
tongue" (Exodus 4:10). Stephen informs us that Moses
was a mighty, powerful speaker. The explanation is that
Moses did not think so; he felt his own utter inability.
Perhaps he had too much of an inferiority complex, for
God appointed Aaron to do the speaking. He was altogether too good a speaker, too ready with his tongue:
witness Exodus 32:21-24. In explaining the worship of
the golden calf Aaron said, "I cast the gold into the fire,
and out came this calf." He talks as if the calf just walked
out of the crucible, but Scripture tells us that he fash-
ioned it with a graving tool, after he had made it a

molten calf (Exodus 32:4). I have found in my life that ready talkers often talk too much, even if not downright lies, or harmful things. Moses' excuses should teach us on the one hand not to be proud; nor on the other hand to excuse ourselves in a false modesty.

Verse 55. Stephen saw Jesus standing on the right hand of God. In other passages we always see Him *sitting down* at the right hand of God. The expression does not mean, of course, that Jesus is always sitting in Heaven. When we say that Queen Elizabeth is on the throne of England, we do not mean that she is always sitting on a throne (I don't believe she ever is), but we mean that she is the reigning monarch. The Bible means exactly the same thing. When we read here that Stephen saw Jesus standing, I believe the suggestion is that the blessed Saviour was standing as it were to welcome the first Christian martyr home to the courts of light above.

Verse 60. How precious to read that Stephen "fell asleep." Stones battered his body, but he fell asleep. No matter how fierce the storm may blow here, for the Christian death is sleep, sleep to be broken in upon when our blessed Lord returns to take His people Home; then those who sleep in Jesus will rise first to meet the Lord in the air.

Verse 58. The witnesses laid down their clothes at the feet of a young man whose name was Saul. Rather ironic, isn't it, that those who batter the life out of a servant of Christ could not trust one another and needed a custodian of their clothes, lest they should rob each other!

Who could have known that, as the enemies of Christ were about to kill God's servant, He had another one right there, eventually to take Stephen's place—one who would outshine any other servant of God ever to come upon the scene. Surely, His ways are past finding out. I suppose Saul of Tarsus was too young at this time, but he got that day the first lesson in an education that was to fit him as God's greatest servant and martyr of Christianity.

Could Saul, later called Paul, ever forget this scene? Like Stephen, he too was to see Jesus of Nazareth in the glory, not at the end of his path of service, but at the beginning. The glory shining in Stephen's face was to shine even brighter in the face of Saul of Tarsus. Yes, when one of God's saints is taken away to glory, God has another prepared to take his place. God buries His workmen but carries on His work. Stephen's graduation was Paul's initiation.

8

Three Conversions

THE CONVERSION of the Ethiopian eunuch in chapter 8, of Saul of Tarsus in chapter 9, and of the Roman centurion Cornelius in chapter 10 seem to be examples to show how the grace of God goes out to all men alike. There are interesting comparisons and contrasts in these outstanding conversions:

1. All three men apparently were moral, upright men; yet they all were lost and needed to be saved.

2. All three had a special messenger sent to speak to them. How shall they hear without a preacher? It is a great privilege to carry the Word of life to sinful souls.

3. One was a black man; another a Jew; the third a Gentile.

4. They represent the whole human race. The Ethiopian was a descendant of Ham; Saul of Shem; and Cornelius of Japheth.

5. The first was a politician—the secretary of Candace's treasury; the second a great theologian; the third a militarist. These three classes are usually the very hardest to reach with the gospel.

6. The first was aroused by reading the Word; the second by seeing and hearing the Lord from glory; the third by an angelic vision.

7. One was on his way home; the second going from home; and the third at home.

8. One was looking for peace and going back home unrewarded in his search; the second was out destroying peace; the third was seeking God's peace.

These three spiritual conditions one meets often. Some, like the eunuch, want to be saved, but don't know how; others, like Saul, are blind to their need in their self-satisfied religious blindness; while many need only to have the message brought to their attention to grasp it by faith immediately, as did Cornelius.

Philip and the Ethiopian Eunuch

ACTS 8

READ THIS whole chapter 8 of Acts; it is most encouraging and challenging.

The gospel is now leaving Judea and reaching the next stage, as the Lord had commanded. In succeeding chapters it goes wider still, to the regions beyond—the uttermost parts of the earth.

The opening verse of the chapter tells us there came great persecution against the church at Jerusalem, consequent to the death of Stephen, and the believers, except the apostles, were scattered through the regions of Judea and Samaria. History shows that later on the apostles too went far afield with the message of God's grace. No doubt their remaining at Jerusalem at this time was of God. They braved the greater dangers at headquarters in Jerusalem, in the very mouth of the lion, as it were; probably they were needed at the center as an authoritative oversight of the work of the Lord. We learn something of this need in Acts 15. While as yet there were no written New Testament Scriptures, the leadership of these men appointed by the Lord as His apostles was greatly needed.

One of those who left Jerusalem and came to Samaria was Philip, mentioned after Stephen in the list of men chosen in Acts 6. Some think this Philip was the one mentioned as one of the Lord's apostles in the Gospels, but this cannot be, for verse 1 states that the apostles did not leave Jerusalem. And further, had Philip been an apostle there would have been no need for Peter and John to come from Jerusalem to impart the Holy Spirit to those saved under Philip's preaching; Philip then would have had that authority himself.

Philip preached Christ, with God's blessing richly attending his preaching. God confirmed his ministry by miracles and signs done by him. Simon the sorcerer himself professed to believe. His conduct afterwards throws doubt on whether he was truly saved or not. Some believe he was a true believer, led astray with a desire for power (true Christians often are afflicted that way today). His humble reply to Peter's strong rebuke—in verse 24—is rather in his favor. In either case, if he was not saved, it is a lesson to sinners to beware of coming so near and yet being so far; if he was truly saved, he ought to point a warning to every one of us, that in our service we might ever seek only the honor and glory of our Lord, and not personal interest or power or greed.

From this happy field of labor and great success, Philip is suddenly called away by the angel of the Lord to travel south on the road that goes from Jerusalem to Gaza—the territory of the Philistines of old. There is a distance of some eighty miles between the cities of Samaria and Gaza, though Philip may not have gone all the way; yet for those days quite a long way. The apostles or other believers in Jerusalem were at least thirty miles closer to the eunuch than was Philip; why didn't the Lord send one of them on this journey? Why take away Philip in the midst of such a time of great harvesting? Who knows? God's ways are not like our ways. It is His to command; the servant's to obey. And Philip did just that. He could learn at least this one lesson, and so can we, that before God none of us are unexpendable. God can and will use whom He will. Philip did God's will cheerfully; he even ran when told to join the eunuch's chariot.

He found one of earth's great men—the treasurer under Candace, Queen of the Ethiopians—returning home rather disconsolate. He had been to Jerusalem, headquarters of the true religion, where God had placed His Name. But he came away as dark spiritually as he had come. One wonders at this, specially because the city was stirred then by the preaching of this new doctrine concerning Jesus of Nazareth. Multitudes there had just recently been saved and many signs and wonders had been done in the Name of Jesus. It seems that too little —or none—of this had reached this politician. Could it be that he, as so many do today, had ignored those who had no recognized place in the religious hierarchy, and had gone instead to the great names in Judaism? Gone to the Temple, which Jehovah had left, and sought light from the blind leaders of the blind? That is what many do now. Few will listen to the humble folk who preach Christ; who, instead of making a name for themselves, seek to lift up the Name which is above every name. Rather they try to "fill their belly with the husks the swine eat," but no man gives to them.

Anyway, this man returned as empty as he came. But at least he brought something worth-while away from Jerusalem—a copy of part, if not the whole, of God's Word. He was reading the prophet Isaiah and it is no mere chance that he was reading the 53d chapter. Philip's text was all ready for him. What better text could any preacher want than Isaiah 53?

"Understandest thou what thou readest?" asks Philip. The eunuch, though a great man, seemed to be a humble one, to his eternal benefit. Pride is the crowning sin that keeps folks from Christ. He replies, "How can I, except some man should guide me?" Then Philip opened his mouth and began at the same Scripture and preached unto him Jesus. He told the story of the Saviour's humiliation and His sacrificial death and no doubt of His glorious exaltation. He may have told him that those who trust the Saviour confess that faith in baptism, for when they came to a certain water the eunuch said: "See, here is water; what doth hinder me to be baptized?" The implication is that, unless he had had faith in Christ, there would have been something to prevent baptism. Only he that believeth is baptized. So Philip baptized him.

Then the Spirit of the Lord caught away Philip, and the new convert went on his way rejoicing. When a soul has truly found Christ, the servant passes out of the picture, that Christ may be all in all.

Philip was found at Azotus and preached all the way north in all the cities till he came to Caesarea. He followed the seacoast north for some seventy-five miles or so, preaching as he went. Note that he did not return to Samaria. He did not become the pastor of the flock at Samaria, but served the Lord as the Holy Spirit directed.

9

The Conversion of Saul of Tarsus

ACTS 9:1-20

THIS IS of such tremendous importance and so stirring, that we are citing the account in full:

"And Saul, yet breathing out threatenings and slaughter against the disciples of the Lord, went unto the high priest, and desired of him letters to Damascus to the synagogues, that if he found any of this way, whether they were men or women, he might bring them bound unto Jerusalem. And as he journeyed, he came near Damascus: and suddenly there shined round about him a light from heaven: And he fell to the earth, and heard a voice saying unto him, Saul, Saul, why persecutest thou Me? And he said, Who art Thou, Lord? And the Lord said, I am Jesus whom thou persecutest: it is hard for thee to kick against the pricks.

"And he trembling and astonished said, Lord, what wilt Thou have me to do? And the Lord said unto him, Arise, and go into the city, and it shall be told thee what thou must do. And the men which journeyed with him stood speechless, hearing a voice, but seeing no man.

"And Saul arose from the earth; and when his eyes

were opened, he saw no man: but they led him by the hand, and brought him into Damascus. And he was three days without sight, and neither did eat nor drink.

"And there was a certain disciple at Damascus named Ananias; and to him said the Lord in a vision, Ananias. And he said, Behold, I am here, Lord. And the Lord said unto him, Arise, and go into the street which is called Straight, and enquire in the house of Judas for one called Saul, of Tarsus: for, behold, he prayeth, And hath seen in a vision a man named Ananias coming in, and putting his hand on him, that he might receive his sight.

"Then Ananias answered, Lord, I have heard by many of this man, how much evil he hath done to Thy saints at Jerusalem: And here he hath authority from the chief priests to bind all that call on Thy name. But the Lord said unto him, Go thy way: for he is a chosen vessel unto Me, to bear My name before the Gentiles, and kings, and the children of Israel: For I will shew him how great things he must suffer for My name's sake.

"And Ananias went his way, and entered into the house; and putting his hands on him said, Brother Saul, the Lord, even Jesus, that appeared unto thee in the way as thou camest, hath sent me, that thou mightest receive thy sight, and be filled with the Holy Ghost. And immediately there fell from his eyes as it had been scales: and he received sight forthwith, and arose, and was baptized.

"And when he had received meat, he was strengthened. Then was Saul certain days with the disciples which were at Damascus. And straightway he preached Christ in the synagogues, that He is the Son of God"—Acts 9:1-20

Paul's conversion is a sample of true Christian conversion. He was saved through a Christ not only crucified, but glorified; and so is every sinner today that is saved. Every detail in connection with the tremendous transformation in his life is full of typical and spiritual significance. Sovereign grace shines forth here in its brightest glory as Paul himself later on declared, saying: "I thank Christ Jesus our Lord, who hath enabled me, for that He counted me faithful, putting me into the ministry; who was before a blasphemer, and a persecutor, and injurious: but I obtained mercy, because I did it ignorantly in unbelief. And the grace of our Lord was exceeding abundant with faith and love which is in Christ Jesus" (1 Timothy 1:12-14). Saul of Tarsus' experience typifies the true, normal salvation of any sinner during this reign of God's grace. He was the first man to be saved by a call from Heaven, a call coming from the risen glorified Lord, and thus he pictures how sinners are saved because the once-rejected Jesus of Nazareth now lives in Heaven, a Prince and a Saviour to give repentance and remission of sins.

What a tale this is—Saul changed into Paul! He was no doubt named after Israel's first king, who stood head and shoulders above the people. So did this namesake of his; only in Paul's case it was morally and intellectually and religiously that he towered over the men of his day. Paul himself describes his moral height as a fiery zealot during the days prior to his conversion, in Philippians 3:4-6. Then he was a big man (in his own eyes as well as in those of his contemporaries), proud, zealous, self-willed. But when his eyes were opened to see himself as God sees, his name was changed to Paul, which means "little." Now he proclaims himself truly to be but little; as he says, "Not meet to be called an apostle; less than the least of all saints; the chief of sinners." Having seen the Lord Jesus in His glory and grace, he himself now shrinks into nothingness. It is so with every truly born-again soul; He must increase but we must decrease.

Saul, breathing out threatenings and slaughter against the disciples of the Lord went to Damascus to arrest and persecute such. It literally reads that he was breathing "in" threatenings and slaughter. He had become as it were a bloodthirsty man-eating tiger in his blinded, false zeal for God. He was a merciless persecutor; but on his way to arrest others, he was himself arrested by Jesus of Nazareth; human cruelty was met by divine mercy. Praise His name, it was grace that arrested this great sinner; grace that ever afterwards became his theme—marvelous, infinite, matchless grace.

A light from Heaven shone, and a voice spoke into Saul's soul. He could boast of being blameless as touching the righteousness in the law, but law-keeping had led him wrongly; it had made him a persecutor of the only Saviour of sinners. The law shuts Heaven against man, but Saul heard the words of grace from an opened Heaven.

> Oh, the glory of the grace
> Shining in the Saviour's face;
> Telling sinners from above:
> God is light and God is love.

Ever after grace became Paul's boast and glory. Out of some one hundred twenty-five times that the word is found in the New Testament, Paul uses it more than one hundred. The Lord sent Ananias to Saul, whose name tells the same wonderful tale, for it means "the Lord has shown grace." Read Galatians 1:15; Romans 3:24; 5:15; 2 Corinthians 8:9; Ephesians 2:8-9; 1 Corinthians 15:10; etc., etc., and you will see how Paul ever after gloried in the grace of God.

The erstwhile persecutor had been plowing his own way, and we read that the plowing of the wicked is sin (Proverbs 21:4). Saul had been kicking against the pricks, which, I understand, oxen did when rebelling against the command of the plowman. In doing so they would only hurt themselves as they kicked their heels into the sharp spikes behind them; so Paul had been hurting himself by resisting the working of God's Spirit. The suggestion here is that God had spoken to his conscience before; perhaps at the stoning of Stephen when he saw his face shining as the face of an angel. Now that he is saved, he is the willing "ox" as he serves, yoked to his Lord. Ananias finds him in the street called "Straight."

Once Saul had been plowing crooked furrows, now he is in the straight and narrow way. Henceforth his purpose in life is expressed in his own words: "One thing I do: I press toward the mark. Not I, but Christ."

Saul is found in the street called Straight, in the house of one Judas. Again, how typical this is! Once he was breathing in murder; now he is breathing out prayer and praise; he is in the house of Judas, whose name means "praise." Both prayer and praise are the outstanding marks of a truly converted soul, and both were so prominent in Paul's afterlife. Often we hear Paul praying; often we hear him burst out in paeans of praise. In the midst of some involved contention or stirring message often we hear him break forth into praise, as in Romans 11:33; 2 Corinthians 9:15; 1 Timothy 1:17; Ephesians 1:3; etc., etc.

Next we find him preaching (verse 20), seeking to turn men from darkness to light and from the power of Satan unto God.

Finally he is being persecuted (verses 23-25). From a persecutor, plowing in sin, we see him prostrate on his face before the Lord on the highway; then praying, praising, preaching, and persecuted.

He is taken by Barnabas (verses 27-28), whose first name is Joseph, to the disciples at Jerusalem and upon his commendation is welcomed by them. Thus he is added (the meaning of the name "Joseph") to the saints to enjoy the privilege of Christian fellowship, and this was a great consolation (the meaning of the name "Barnabas") both to him and to them.

The Lord, speaking to the sinner Saul from Heaven, said to him: "Why persecutest thou Me?" *Thou—Me*. Actually Saul had been persecuting the saints, but Jesus reminds him that He and His saints are one, which is the blessed truth of the Church, the Body of Christ, of which the Lord is the Head; the truth of which Paul later was to unfold so wonderfully. Like his blessed Lord, Paul too nourished and cherished the Church and in a lesser degree gave himself for it.

A number of thoughts—in a practical strain—suggest themselves in the conversion of this great servant of Christ. Everything about it is great: the man who was saved; the manner of his salvation; the world-shaking results therefrom.

1. His conversion tells how fearfully wrong man can be, yet think at the same time that he is absolutely right. Religion has a peculiar soporific effect on men.

2. It tells us that the most hopeless case is not hopeless. Ananias felt that Saul of Tarsus was beyond the reach of God, but the gospel is the power of God.

3. It points the suddenness of true conversion: one moment a mad persecutor, the next a humble penitent.

4. It stresses man's insignificance. How little this big Saul was, after all. The proud man falls helpless to the ground; he trembles in astonishment. From a haughty, fiery zealot to a poor, groveling sinner in a moment. Man is pretty small when he is in the presence of God.

5. It teaches the marvelous grace of God. There is not a word of rebuke; no reminding this sinner of his awful

guilt; just a gentle question that searches and humbles him. Seeing Jesus of Nazareth, whom he had believed to be an impostor, actually on the throne of God in Heaven totally smashed all his former unbelief.

6. In opposing God, Saul learned, he had really been hindering his own blessing. It is hard to kick against the pricks. Says God: "Who will contend with Me?"

7. This might have been Saul's last chance. Had he refused now, it might well have been forever too late. But Paul was not disobedient to the heavenly vision. It is true that we are not shown a vision as Saul saw it, but this is not needed. We have the sure record of Scripture that He who once hung on the cross is now seated on the throne of God. Before Him every knee must bow.

8. This conversion stresses the sovereignty of God. The Lord on this occasion saved just this one man. Paul alone heard the voice speaking to him; he alone was blinded by the light. When the Lord speaks to your soul, do not fail to heed His voice!

9. Paul was to suffer great things for Jesus' sake (verse 16). Unto us, on behalf of Christ, it is given not only to believe on Him, but also to suffer for His sake (Philippians 1:29).

I should like to mention that this new convert Saul (afterwards known as Paul), like all servants whom God would use in His service, needed a time of retirement for meditation, prayer, and communion with God. One might think, reading Acts 9:20, that Paul began to preach immediately after he was saved, but Galatians

1:17 shows this is not so. He went into Arabia for three years, returning from there to Damascus. Those three years must be read between the lines between Acts 9:19 and 20, in the light of Galatians 1:17. It is upon Paul's return from Arabia to Damascus that he began to preach there, as Acts 9:20 states. Escaping from that city, upon the threat of being killed (verse 23), he came to Jerusalem. This must be so, for Paul tells us in Galatians 1:18 that he did not get to Jerusalem till three years after his conversion.

From Jerusalem, according to Acts 9:30, the brethren sent Paul to Tarsus, and from thence Barnabas brought him to Antioch, as recorded in Acts 11:25-26. This was at least eight to nine years after Paul's sojourn in Arabia, for it was from Antioch that Paul and Barnabas returned to the famous council at Jerusalem, given in Acts 15. Paul tells us in Galatians 2:1 that this was fourteen years after he had been in Jerusalem before. Thus from the time Paul was saved we find him three years in Arabia, say nine years in Tarsus (his home town), and about two years laboring in Antioch with Barnabas, which makes the total of fourteen years between Paul's first and second visit to Jerusalem; or, which is the same thing, between his conversion and his coming to Jerusalem as seen in Galatians 2:1 and Acts 15, which both refer to the same occasion.

I mention this to show that Paul was out of the public eye for about 12 years after he was saved till he entered into what we call today "full time service for the Lord." All these years were spent in preparation for his life's

work. If this gifted servant of Christ needed this school-
ing, so does every preacher today. Many are too ready
to start out telling others before they know much yet
themselves. Moses had forty years of college in the desert; Elisha humbly waited on Elijah as a common slave,
to be fitted to take up where his master left off. Elijah
himself went on a lonely forty-day walk to learn some
things. The greatest Preacher of all spent thirty years in
obscurity.

Let us look at Saul's conversion once more as follows:

Captured. He was apprehended by divine love. He
persecuted men to death; love pursued him to bring him
life eternal. Instead of putting others to death, Paul's
Saviour and ours was put to death for the sins of others.
Love puts its hand on Saul of Tarsus and says: "I arrest
you; you are henceforth the Lord's prisoner; a captive
of love."

Conquered. Many a criminal in prison has been captured; not so many are conquered. Their wills are still
unyielded. But Paul could say: "I was not disobedient
to the heavenly vision." Like His Lord he too could say:
"I delight to do Thy will."

Captivated. Paul's heart was won. His whole soul
became engrossed with the loveliness of Him who saved
him. All he once boasted in he now counted but loss for
Christ. He found in Jesus not only the superexcellency
of knowledge that challenges the mind, but a love that
satisfied every craving of his ransomed soul.

Controlled. The love of Christ constrained him henceforth not to live for himself but unto Him who died for him and rose again. That he might bring honor and glory to Christ became his consuming passion.

Have Thine own way Lord; have Thine own way,
    Hold o'er my being absolute sway;
Fill with Thy Spirit till all shall see,
    Christ only, always, living in me.

Two Miracles by Simon Peter

ACTS 9:32-43

CHRIST WAS rejected and crucified; the first Christian martyr, Stephen, is stoned to death; and still Israel continues to refuse God's mercy and seeks to crush the witness to Christ. In verse 29 of this chapter they seek to kill Saul and the brethren send him away to Tarsus. Odd to read in verse 31 that "then had the churches rest throughout all Judea and Galilee and Samaria." Paul's witness for Christ must have irritated his enemies intensely, for his disappearance seems to allay the persecution completely for a while. The churches were edified and, walking in the fear of the Lord and in the comfort of the Holy Ghost, were multiplied.

Note that in verse 31 here we read for the first time in Acts of "churches" outside of Jerusalem. It tells us that the saints were being gathered together entirely outside of Judaism and that assemblies of saints met throughout the whole of the land of Israel. And all this before the truth in connection with the Church was revealed to Paul or revealed by Paul. The Holy Spirit was working to gather out of the world a people for His Name. We are getting away, in this historical account in the Acts, from the superintendency of Jerusalem or any connection with the Temple (where the saints met at first), and we see assemblies of believers meeting after the New Testament pattern, later made known in detail through Paul's ministry.

Now, for the first time, also in Acts, we read of one of the apostles—Peter—going further afield, as the other apostles did likewise later on, according to tradition. Many that dwelt at Lydda and Sharon turned to the Lord. Sharon is a plain stretching from Joppa north toward Caesarea along the seacoast, the very route Philip had followed, as we saw in our study of chapter 8. Peter follows now in the wake of the evangelist, under the guidance of the Spirit. As a result of the miracle Peter performs, all the people of that region turned to the Lord (verse 35); there is a similar happy result in Joppa (verse 42). One wonders whether Philip's preaching of the gospel had not prepared this soil for the ready response under Peter's ministry.

There is an evident similarity between the miracles of this chapter and those done by the Lord Himself. Peter seems to have learned methods from his Master, whom we also do well to imitate. In the case of Aeneas, Peter tells him to arise and make his bed, as Jesus told the man who was borne of four to take up his bed and walk. In the case of Dorcas, raised from the dead, the details are similar to those at the raising of Jairus' daughter. In both, the bystanders are put out; both are raised up by being taken by the hand. And, as the miracles are somewhat alike, so is their dispensational meaning. Israel may reject God's mercy, but God's grace flows on, as is seen typically, I believe, in these two miracles. God hath not cast away His people. Aeneas, a paralytic unable to walk, well pictures Israel that so utterly failed to live for God's glory. His name means "praise," but praise here is paralyzed. However, by divine grace and power this shall be changed with Israel in the future, as it was with this man here. The miracle happened at Lydda, which means "birth" or "travail." Israel's new birth, her travail—see Isaiah 66:8-10—shall yet make her a praise in all the earth (Zephaniah 3:20). Aeneas having been paralyzed eight years suggests that Israel's salvation will truly be the mark of a spiritual resurrection, for the number eight is the number speaking of a new beginning.

In the raising of Dorcas a similar story is told. As far as being God's people is concerned, at present Israel is dead, yet He has not cast them off permanently. In the raising of this saint is foreshadowed the happy future of the Jewish people. God looks at Israel in two ways: in their perversion and rebellion against Him He can only say of them, "Lo-ammi—not My people," but from the viewpoint of His eternal purposes regarding them, He sees them as still His own; He remembers how they went after Him in the wilderness (Jeremiah 2:2-3), and because of His promises to the fathers, He will yet bless them. Dorcas lived at Joppa, which means "fair to Him," and this well expresses how He sees His own in grace.

Dorcas' name is given both in Hebrew and Greek; both having the same meaning. The basic meaning is "beauty," with the secondary translation "gazelle," an animal noted for its beauty. The word is found, I think, five times in the Old Testament. How wonderful to think that Israel is beautiful in His sight, even as we too are accepted in the Beloved. For Israel there awaits a spiritual new birth; an awakening from spiritual death as Tabitha was roused from physical death. Here, as in the healing of Aeneas, as a result many believed in the Lord. It will be so in Israel's future day; vast numbers of Gentiles will turn to Christ as the result of Israel's rebirth and they shall share Israel's blessing during Christ's millennial and eternal reign.

10

Priming the Preacher

ACTS 10:1-23

PETER WITH the other apostles at first stayed in Jerusalem. Then—as seen in chapter 8—he came to Samaria to impart the Holy Spirit to those Samaritans who had trusted Christ. In our last chapter, we find him going out still further, though as yet moving among and ministering to the Jews only. However, the Lord had chosen him to use the keys to the kingdom of heaven. He did so in relation to Israel in Acts 2, and is now called to do the same in the case of Cornelius, in relation to the Gentiles. As Peter says in Acts 15:7: "God made choice among us, that the Gentiles by my mouth should hear the word of the gospel, and believe."

But Peter was a Jew, with all the strong prejudices of the race, and he was not easily made to open his eyes to see God's purpose and God's will. First God gave Cornelius, the Roman centurion, a vision of an angel instructing him to send to Joppa and call for Simon, whose surname is Peter. Next, God gives Peter a vision of the sheet let down from heaven, in order to prepare him and make him ready to go with the messengers sent to fetch him. The Lord God did not employ an angel to speak to Cornelius the message of grace; this great privilege is committed to sinners saved by grace. An angel speaks to Cornelius, the Lord speaks to Peter, and Peter finally preached to Cornelius. How wonderful that our Lord uses us to tell the story, even though often we, like Peter, are so slow to obey orders.

While the messengers were on their journey from Caesarea, Peter, while praying on the housetop around noon and becoming very hungry, fell into a trance. He saw in a vision heaven opened and a sheet, knit at the four corners, descending. In it were four different kinds of animals, including insects and birds. A voice said: "Rise Peter, kill and eat." Peter (very illogically, as it is so often with us) said: "Not so, Lord." "Not so" and "Lord" are flat contradictions. If He is Lord, you cannot say "No" to His orders. Peter says: "I have never eaten any thing common or unclean." And the voice from Heaven came back: "What God hath cleansed, that call not thou common." This was done three times over. Peter's history carries a number of three's: three times he denied the Lord; three times the Lord challenged Peter's love (John 21); and now three times another lesson is repeated. At first Peter did not understand the meaning of the vision, but later he recognized that in the sight of God (Acts 10:28) there is no difference between the Jew and the Gentile, "for the same Lord over all is rich unto all that call upon Him" (Romans 10:12).

The great sheet let down from an open heaven, with its conglomerate contents, seems to illustrate the truth concerning the Church—God's dealings in this day of grace:

1. It comes from an open heaven, which is typical of

the day in which we live. Christ went into Heaven, and opened its portals to us (Hebrews 10:19).

2. The *great* sheet suggests the vast outreach of the gospel of God's grace in this day, wherein millions have been won to Christ.

3. Knit at the "four corners" suggests that God's grace goes out world-wide.

4. Those whom God saves are from the two prominent classes in the world as God sees them—the Jews and the Gentiles. The Jews are seen in this net as the beasts of the "earth"—tame beasts—as Israel had been educated in God's moral laws. The term "earth" is consistently used in Scripture in connection with Israel. The "wild beasts" picture the lawless Gentiles (they are seen as wild beasts in Daniel's visions), while the creeping things speak of the low passions that mark sinners, and the "fowls of the air" are a familiar figure standing for the operation of satanic influence. Thus the whole cargo pictures Jew and Gentile alike by nature subject to the evil lusts of the flesh and the wiles of the devil. It is such the grace of God blesses. All being together in the same sheet suggests that there is no difference between Jew and Gentile; all alike are sinners (Romans 3:22-23); all alike are subjects of the grace of God (Romans 10:12).

5. Peter said he had never eaten anything common or unclean. He meant by "common" that which the unclean Gentiles ate; by the laws of God the Jew had been set apart from them and could not take any common stand with them; it would defile him (the same word here given as *common* is translated *defiled* in Mark 7:2).

But the Cross has leveled all men, declared the whole world guilty before God; so that all sinners alike are on one common level. And, as they are alike guilty, so the grace of God reaches them alike; and when saved by grace, they are no longer common with the world, no longer defiled in His sight or their own. So God says to him: "What God hath cleansed, that call not thou common."

Now, praise God, Peter was common in a new way; common with the Gentile in a happy holy communion of saints. (The word *communion* is the noun of the adverb *common* used here.) Now believers have all things common, but no longer with the world; only with fellow saints. Now all those, once vile sinners in this great sheet, as it were, including Peter and Cornelius, are cleansed by the precious blood of Christ, as the Lord was teaching Peter by this vision.

6. The sheet came from heaven and was received up again into heaven, telling us that the Church's origin is heavenly, and so is her destiny. Some day all the myriads of believers shall be caught up into Heaven, as this sheet was received up. Praise His Name!

Peter Goes to Cornelius' Home

ACTS 10:23-33

As PETER enters Cornelius' home, that centurion—a Roman—fell down at his feet and worshiped him. Millions of Romans (Roman Catholics) have since then bowed at the feet of him whom they claim is Peter's successor—the Pope—but now, as then, without Peter's consent. To venerate and adore religiously a human being is idolatry, and Peter would have none of it.

"Stand up," said he, "I myself also am a man." To worship anyone but the living God is vile wickedness, and flatly refused here by Peter.

He finds many gathered together (verse 27), a truly God-prepared audience ready to hear all the apostle had to tell them. Cornelius was really in earnest, for not only was he himself prepared to hear the Word of God, but he had filled his house with invited guests—many of them. What a thrill for any preacher to speak to a group like that! No wonder the Holy Ghost fell in divine power on such an audience. Peter briefly explains why he has come and Cornelius rehearses the circumstances that caused him to send for Peter. After these preliminaries, all are ready for the first sermon preached to a wholly Gentile audience.

Peter's Sermon

ACTS 10:34-48

PETER'S SERMON is a marvel of simplicity, yet of great comprehensiveness. He gives a brief summation of the Lord's ministry from the announcement of Him by John the Baptist, telling of His works of mercy and power (verses 36-38); then goes on to speak of His crucifixion and resurrection—a resurrection attested to by His own redeemed ones who saw Him after He rose from the dead (verses 39-41). He reminds them that the Old Testament Jewish prophets had foretold all these things concerning the Saviour; now—through this Man—whosoever believes in Him shall receive remission of sins. Peter's message was plain, powerful, and persuasive.

Right in the middle of the sermon the Holy Ghost fell on all who heard the Word. What a blessed way to have a meeting interrupted! I have seen this myself a few times in my life, and would love to see more of it. The Jews were astonished that on the Gentiles also was poured out the gift of the Holy Ghost, that they spoke with tongues. It was, as it were, a second little Pentecost, telling us that Gentiles as well as Jews shared alike in the coming of the Holy Spirit to indwell believers and to unite them into one Body—the Church. Says Peter: "Can any man forbid water, that these should not be baptized, which have received the Holy Ghost as well as we?"

Here is the Christian formula: hearing the Word, believing on Christ to the salvation of the soul, the impartation of the Holy Spirit, baptism in water.

We may note that Peter "commanded them to be baptized" (verse 48). I am not aware that the Scripture lays the responsibility to be baptized on the believer; it lays it on the one through whom such are brought to Christ. Peter took the responsibility here; the disciples in Matthew 28:19 were told to do the baptizing. Preachers have the responsibility to see to it that those saved through their ministry are baptized.

We might note once more the difference between this Gentile Pentecost and the Jewish Pentecost of Acts 2. Here, unlike there, there is no mention of "repent"; no telling them to be baptized; no promise of the Holy Ghost. In Acts 2 the Jews were told to repent in view of their guilt in the crucifixion of their Messiah; they were told to be baptized, as an outward proof of their repentance, and consequent to those two actions they were promised the Holy Spirit. In Acts 10 on the contrary the Holy Spirit falls on these believers without any promise of His coming being given, and baptism is not here the evidence of repentance but of "faith."

In fact, in full-blown Christianity, repentance is not mentioned in connection with salvation, as it is not here in our subject. John's Gospel, which is the Christian gospel of the four Gospels, never once mentions repentance, but has "believe" many, many times. The Christian message is "believe," not "repent." When told to repent one will look at "self" naturally; when told to believe, one looks at another—at *Christ*. Of course, looking to Christ for salvation, one repents at the same time, for it is because one knows self to be sinful and lost that one will turn to Christ. But the emphasis is on "believing"; and it is so here in Acts 10.

II

Simon Peter Rehearses

ACTS 11:1-18

PETER GIVES an account of his going to Cornelius' home and what transpired there. There were many Jews in Jerusalem as prejudiced as Peter himself had been. Peter knew this, and very wisely had taken six witnesses along with him (verse 12). As he rehearses the mighty grace of God to the Gentiles, his hearers are satisfied; they glorify God; and it begins to dawn upon their hearts that the infinite God cannot limit His love to one tiny little nation. God's heart takes in the whole world, for God so loved the world that He gave His only begotten Son.

Thus another step is taken—from the narrow confines of Judaism into the world-wide regions where the story of divine love would yet be told so fully. Peter here opens to the Gentiles the door into which another—the Apostle Paul—would enter to introduce the great and wondrous truths of Christianity, of the Church of God. We are given one more look at Peter, after which he disappears from the record of the book of Acts; in a similar manner John the Baptist was removed after the Lord Jesus appeared upon the scene. God fulfils His purposes of infinite grace and uses whom He will and where He will.

The question is often raised as to whether or not Cornelius was a believer when he sent for Peter, and opinion is widely divergent on that point. Peter's statement in verse 14 of Acts 11 is pointed out, where he says that Cornelius was to send for Peter "who shall tell thee words, whereby thou and all thy house shall be saved." This sounds like clear proof that Cornelius was *not* saved at that time. However, in chapter 10 Cornelius states in verse 6 that the angel told him "Peter . . . shall tell thee what thou oughtest to do"; again in verse 32 of chapter 10 the angel uses the words "Peter . . . when he cometh, shall speak unto thee." In neither of these two verses does Cornelius hear or say anything about being "saved." To me it is apparent that Peter himself gives that interpretation to the angel's words. Being a prejudiced Jew, he could not conceive of anyone being saved except a Jew. Yet he ought to have known better, for many Gentiles—even in the record of the Old Testament—were saved, including their famous father Abraham. For myself, I believe that Cornelius was a saved man (I don't see how else one could account for verses 2 and 4 of chapter 10), but one who had never heard the gospel of God's grace, and who was by its preaching introduced into the Church. I believe the emphasis in this whole story is not so much the conversion of these people as the truth that here the Gentiles were added to the Church as were the Jews in Acts 2.

Christians First at Antioch

ACTS 11:19-30

Now WE see the grace of God going forth still further
to the Gentiles. At first the gospel is preached to the
Jews only (verse 19), but then a largely Gentile church
is formed at Antioch (see Acts 15:3), which hereafter
assumes, we might say, the status of headquarters for
the going forth of the gospel to the regions beyond.
The disciples were called Nazarenes at Jerusalem; now
in Antioch they are called Christians for the first time.

Antioch means "over against," and it is in its spiritual
impact that it stands over against Jerusalem; not in opposition, but in contrast. In Jerusalem we have divinely
instituted authority and control in the twelve apostles,
but here we see the free action of the Holy Spirit in using
the humblest believer in the service of the Lord. It is a
true foreshadowing of the Church as we see its constitu-
tion in Scripture. There is no officialism in Antioch; here
are no big names—just humble believers, carrying the
gospel as they go.

All through the Church's history this pattern should
have been followed. God's Word in the New Testament
knows nothing of a controlling board or central power;
knows nothing of human ordination or of appointment
by man to preach. Though Paul is raised up as God's
special servant, he never assumes any authority over

the consciences or liberty of the saints; the ministry of Christ is the right and the responsibility of every believer.

A great number believed and turned to the Lord (verse 21). The Church at Jerusalem hears of this and sends out Barnabas. When he came he was glad to see God working so mightily; he exhorted the young believers to cleave to the Lord with purpose of heart, and through his ministry many more were saved (verse 24).

Then comes a truly lovely note. Barnabas departed to Tarsus to seek Saul. He knew him well; had introduced him to the leaders in Jerusalem after his conversion. Paul had retired to his home town for, as we saw in chapter 9 of Acts, perhaps eight to nine years. Barnabas, without an envious bone in his body, felt that while he himself might do as a preacher or an exhorter, these young converts needed teaching and Barnabas knew just the man to do it—Saul of Tarsus; and so went after him. How good to realize one's own limitations, and to desire, at the risk of playing second fiddle, only the blessing of God's people for His glory.

The two remained at Antioch a whole year, and the disciples became known as "Christians." It is not clear whether the enemy called them that, or whether it was a designation the believers themselves favored. But it is blessed to be named after Him, blessed to acknowledge that His Name is all-sufficient, that there is no need to take any other.

In the closing verses of chapter 11 we read for the first time of prophets and elders in the Church. All this intimates that the Church was gradually taking shape as God's witness on earth, with the various gifts and qualifications needed for its testimony present. Elsewhere we read that prophets as well as apostles formed the foundation of the Church, and that elders were appointed by the Holy Spirit to look after the spiritual needs of the saints.

Antioch in Syria was situated about three hundred miles north of Jerusalem, and sixteen miles from the sea. It became the base of operations for Paul's life work. It is believed that Agabus made his prophecy of the coming famine in A.D. 44, and that it actually did come two years later. Paul came out of retirement into full and uninterrupted service for his Lord approximately twelve or more years after our Lord's death.

12

Last Mention of Peter

THE LAST eight words of this portion (verse 17) read: "And he [Peter] departed, and went into another place." That is truly descriptive of Peter's disappearance from the page of history. We see no more of him in the book of Acts; he has departed and gone to another place but where that place is, nobody knows. The Roman Catholic Church says he came to Rome, but there is not the slightest proof for that claim. He disappears and for a good reason. The ministry of Paul—the truth concerning the Church—takes prominence in this day of grace in the mind of God, though alas, so few even true believers know or care much about this. We profit of course by Peter's written ministry, but Paul's ministry is that which concerns the Church as such.

James is killed by cruel Herod, while God goes to a great deal of trouble to rescue Peter. We cannot always understand God's ways; that is why the Lord Jesus told His disciples when He left: "Ye believe in God, believe also in Me." The Christian must tread the path of faith; not of sight or reason. God has His own all-wise purposes to fulfil and He doeth all things well. (Later on in this book we will look in detail at lessons we may learn from Peter's deliverance.)

The Death of Herod

THE DEATH of Herod pictures, I believe, a foreshadowing of Israel's future. Having refused their own King, they are now under the rule of a wilful, wicked king—a picture of the future Antichrist. Herod is reigning over the whole land, from north to south, as will be true of the coming wilful king in Israel's future. Herod accepts the worship that is due to God alone and not to any mere man, as so clearly will be arrogated by the Antichrist—as we see in 2 Thessalonians 2:4. As it will be then, so it is here—God's judgment falls on the sinner suddenly, while the Word of God will continue to grow and multiply.

13

The First Missionary Journey

ACTS 13:1-3

WE READ in Acts 12:25 that Paul and Barnabas returned
from Jerusalem, perhaps after taking the relief there sent
by the saints in Antioch, as intimated in chapter 11:29-30.
From Jerusalem they brought with them Mark, who
later on deserted them, because of which Paul and Barnabas separated eventually. Yet Mark, this failing servant,
was selected by the Holy Spirit to write his account of
Christ as God's perfect Servant. And, years later, Paul
himself acknowledges Mark's restoration, and desires his
company. Thus grace triumphs over man's most grievous
failures. How this should encourage any and all of God's
servants!

Acts 13 opens with a new departure. As gradually
the great truths of the Church are to be unveiled, Jerusalem fades into the background, as our Lord Himself said
would be (John 4:21). Antioch, in Gentile territory,
becomes Paul's headquarters, and Judaism fades more
and more into the distance. The Holy Ghost separates
Paul and Barnabas for their special missionary enterprise.

The laying on of hands of those present (verse 3) of
course does not mean they ordained them to the ministry.

Both had been recognized ministers of the Word for years. And certainly the prophets and teachers in Antioch could have no authority whatever to ordain an "apostle." Here is the true simplicity of Christian teaching. They prayed, then laid their hands on these servants of Christ as an expression of their fellowship with them in their work. The Holy Ghost appointed them and empowered them.

Elymas the Sorcerer

ACTS 13:4-12

PAUL AND BARNABAS preached to the Jews first (verse 5). It says nothing as to what reception their message met. But in the conversion of the Gentile deputy Sergius Paulus and the opposition by the Jew Bar-jesus we have a startling picture of the truth enunciated by Paul in 1 Thessalonians 2:15-16. Speaking of the Jews he says: "Who both killed the Lord Jesus, and their own prophets, and have persecuted us; and they please not God, and are contrary to all men: Forbidding us to speak to the Gentiles that they might be saved, to fill up their sins alway: for the wrath is come upon them to the uttermost." Having rejected Christ for themselves is not enough; they will also try to hinder the Gentiles from turning to God.

Bar-jesus stands for the Jewish nation, apostate and trying to turn others away from Christ. Bar-jesus is a false prophet and a sorcerer. He has given himself over to Satan, for Paul calls him a "child of the devil"—the very same term the Lord Jesus applied to the Pharisees that hated and rejected Him (John 8:44). This Bar-jesus spells in his attitude the continued opposition of the Jew to Christ. It is this conflict with the Jew, to which Paul's teaching concerning the Church is so directly antagonistic, that is connected with the change of his name from Saul to Paul. No longer the big Jewish name but the little one as Christ's humble servant.

Bar-jesus is struck blind, as has happened to Israel in a spiritual way. But this blindness, we are told, was only "for a season" (verse 11). So with the nation. "Blindness in part [that is, for a time only] is happened to Israel, until the fulness of the Gentiles be come in" (Romans 11:25). Thus Bar-jesus' judgment sets forth Israel's spiritual blindness because of her sins, but also her future restoration, for it is only for a season.

Paul's Stirring Sermon in Antioch of Pisidia

ACTS 13:13-41

THE SAD spiritual state of Israel is further declared in Paul's sermon in the synagogue in this city. Read it; it is a most impressive charge. As to substance, it is very much like Stephen's address to the council in Jerusalem, and somewhat like Peter's on the day of Pentecost. As did Stephen, so Paul goes over Israel's history, though in much briefer form; nor does he call attention to their treatment of Joseph and Moses, the saviors of those days. Paul mentions something I don't think is found anywhere else in Scripture—the fact that King Saul reigned forty years.

This additional information tells us that the three kings who reigned over the whole twelve tribes—Saul, David, and Solomon—all reigned forty years. In Saul's reign we see the truth given in the Old Testament, the reign of man in the flesh—the reign of sin. In David's reign we have the reign of Christ as the rejected King, while a usurper for a time occupied the throne rightly his—thus picturing the present day of grace. Solomon's reign pictures the future day of glory, the millennium, when our blessed Lord will reign in power and glory.

Thus, in the reigns of these three kings we have a pictorial view of the whole of human history. Number forty in Scripture is the number of testing, so we see in Saul's reign, man tested under law, which produced the works of the flesh; under David, man tested in this day of grace; and pictured in Solomon's reign, man tested in the millennial day and proving then, as now, a failure. Each of these periods closed or will close in judgment. Without God's marvelous grace, what a poor thing man is!

Paul, as did Peter at Pentecost, reminds his Jewish

hearers that the Christ they refused God has raised from the dead, and he quotes the same Old Testament passage for proof (Acts 13:35-37). As Peter did, Paul offers them forgiveness of sins through Christ in the well-known words that "through this man is preached unto you the forgiveness of sins: and by Him all that believe are justified from all things, from which ye could not be justified by the law of Moses" (verses 38-39). Then, as did Stephen, Paul drives home a warning of the judgment that awaits those who despise and wonder and perish. Compare Acts 7:51-53 with Acts 13:40-41.

Neither here nor in Acts 7 is there any offer made to the nation of a kingdom or anything else. Though the nation as a whole is set aside, this does not mean that God's mercy is limited. The offer of salvation is made to any individual who will accept the Saviour. Paul himself assures us in Romans 11:1 that God has not cast away His people. Paul himself is an Israelite, and he has been saved by the grace of God. He ever longed for his brethren after the flesh (Romans 10:1).

The Reaction to Paul's Message

ACTS 13:42-51

AFTER THE Jews in the synagogue had heard the message, the Gentiles besought that these words might be preached to them the next Sabbath. Many Jews that day apparently received God's Word into their hearts (verse 43) for the preachers urged them to continue in the grace of God.

The next Sabbath almost the whole city came together to hear (verse 44). This aroused the rage of the unbelieving Jews, and when they contradicted and blasphemed, Paul and Barnabas tell them that, if they judged themselves unworthy of everlasting life, they would turn to the Gentiles (verse 46). That is what the Lord had told him to do, to begin with, and it is noticeable that in Acts 9:15—at his conversion—Paul had been ordered to bear the Lord's Name before the Gentiles and kings and the children of Israel. The Lord put the Gentiles first and Israel last. Paul reversed the Lord's order, mainly, I believe, because of his passionate love of his own race. But that love of his was largely rewarded by hatred, persecution, and eventually death. We read of persecution in this chapter (verse 50), but when the Gentiles heard the gospel "they were glad and glorified the word of the Lord: and as many as were ordained to eternal life believed."

This whole chapter is a panoramic view of Israel's rejection of Christ (to be repeated again and again in the following chapters); of the gospel's going out ever more widely to the Gentiles through him who was chosen of the Lord to reach those "afar off." Israel rejected the Saviour, but the disciples were filled with joy and with the Holy Ghost (verse 52).

14

The Gospel Preached at Iconium

ACTS 14:1-7

THOUGH JUST PERSECUTED, so great is Paul's desire to see his own people blessed that again he goes first—in Iconium—into the synagogue to preach to the Jews. Here they meet with similar hatred and persecution as at Antioch and as subsequently in Lystra, where Paul was left for dead. Writing later to Timothy (2 Timothy 3:11), Paul refers to those very days of satanic fury: "Persecutions, afflictions, which came unto me at Antioch, at Iconium, at Lystra; what persecutions I endured: but out of them all the Lord delivered me."

Amidst the strong opposition the Lord works mightily and a great multitude of the Jews and also of the Greeks believed. That little word "so" in verse 1 is significant; they "so" spake that a great multitude believed. It is not only important to preach the Word but the "how" is important as well. No doubt they spoke with intense earnestness and a deep longing for the salvation of their hearers. I believe that today we might put a little more emphasis on the "how" of our ministry.

You have heard the tale of the little boy who was asked which was heavier—a pound of feathers or a pound of lead. Without hesitation he replied that of course a pound of lead was the heavier. His questioner laughed at his ignorance. But a short while after, the man who had asked him the question was standing beneath the window of this boy's home. So the lad went upstairs, got a feather pillow from a bed and then a lead weight. First he dropped the pillow on the man's head, then the piece of lead, and said: "Now you tell me which is heavier—a pound of feathers or a pound of lead!" Oh yes, theoretically they weigh the same, but not actually. The lead is heavier because it is concentrated into a more compact form and thus falls with increased force. Even so our ministry is more effective if it comes with spiritual passion and divine power and freshness.

The resistance in Iconium was stronger, and proportionately the manifestation of divine power too was greater, for signs and wonders were done by the hands of the apostles (Barnabas also is here called an apostle). The Lord confirmed by these miracles the truth these men were preaching, establishing the disciples on the one hand and increasing the persecution, aroused by envy, on the other. The servants of Christ, because of a threatened assault with intent to kill them, flee to the cities of Derbe and Lystra.

The Healing of an Impotent Man at Lystra

ACTS 14:8-11

A MIRACLE was performed which the Holy Spirit has seen fit to record on the page of inspiration: the miracle of a lame man being healed. This healing is quite similar to the one recorded in chapter 3, there done by Peter and John. Both these men had been unable to walk from their mother's womb; both had faith to be healed; both, when healed, leaped and walked. Both these miracles, as well as the one by the Lord Himself in John 5, picture Israel, spiritually impotent because of departure from God. Each portrays that some day Israel shall be cured when it turns to the Lord; then the lame man shall leap as the hart. The Jews were violently rejecting Christ then, as seen so prominently in chapters 13 and 14, but God in His mercy interjects an account of this miracle as a beam of divine light and blessing in the sad darkness. Unbelieving Israel shall yet one day have faith; shall one day leap for joy when saved from her impotence by the coming Saviour and Messiah.

Persecution by Israel—Adoration by the Gentiles

ACTS 14:11-18

ON THE PART of the Gentiles this miracle leads to adoration of the apostles, while on the part of the Jews it leads to increasing violence.

Paul's remonstrance to these heathen at Lystra is very simple, and suitable to the occasion, seeing they were idolators. He does not speak to them of the spiritual truths of Christianity, as the death, resurrection, and ascension of Christ, but reminds them that God is the Creator and the Beneficent Giver of every blessing and that therefore worship is due to Him alone. The very witness of God as Creator ought to make men turn from the vanities of life to the living God.

Paul Stoned at Lystra

ACTS 14: 19-28

THE JEWS in their envious malice come from as far away as Antioch in Pisidia and from Iconium and stir up the citizens of Lystra to stone Paul, leaving him lying for dead (verse 19). But to the great amazement of the sorrowing disciples, in spite of the cruel battering of stones, Paul rises up and goes into the city, as though nothing untoward had happened; and the next day he leaves for Derbe. Even if he was not killed, the fearful barrage of stones would ordinarily have incapacitated any man from going about his business; God manifestly performed a miracle.

Many commentators see here possibly the incident of which Paul speaks in 2 Corinthians 12, where he was caught up to the third Heaven. Paul twice tells us that he was not sure whether he was in the body or out of the

body—in other words, whether he was physically alive
or dead. If this be the occasion, then the stoning at Lystra took Paul's life from him and God miraculously
restored him back from death. If Paul was not killed
here at Lystra, then this incident cannot be connected
with that experience of 2 Corinthians 12, for the disciples
here stood around Paul's body, and so he could not have
gone to Heaven *in* his body, for they saw his body lying
there in the street outside of Lystra.

The lesson we may learn from this happening is that
Paul must have been greatly encouraged in his service,
since it proves that nothing can deter a servant of Christ
from the work of the Lord, until the Lord says so. It
proves truly that "our times are in His hand." Verse 21
well shows how Paul learned that blessed truth, for, in
spite of the murderous assault made upon him at Lystra,
after preaching in Derbe, he goes right back to Lystra,
Iconium, and Antioch, where his bitterest enemies lived
and where he had suffered so much at their hands. Knowing God's overruling power, he could well assure the
disciples in that region that "we must through much
tribulation enter into the kingdom of God" (verse 22).

One notable and important feature of Paul's ministry
is seen in verse 23. He organized his work for permanent
fruit by forming churches, or assemblies, in every place,
and taking care there were elders able to look after the
flock of God. This is the double ministry of every servant of Christ—to see souls saved and then to establish
them in the truths concerning Church fellowship and
responsibility.

After passing through the provinces of Pisidia and Pamphylia and preaching in two more cities—Perga and Attalia—they sailed back to Antioch, from whence they had been recommended to the grace of God for the work which they fulfilled. And when they were come and had gathered the church together, they had a special missionary meeting and rehearsed all that God had done with them, and how He had opened the door of faith unto the Gentiles.

Thus ended Paul's first missionary journey, described in the two chapters we have just considered. It is a thrilling story of God's mercy against man's malice; of the forming of assemblies and the fuming of the enemy. Then, as now, the preaching of Christ does not meet with universal success. The devil is a wily foe and stirs in the human heart hatred of God and His truth; while the Holy Spirit woos the souls of men by the matchless love of Christ. "Blessed are all they that put their trust in Him."

15

The Council at Jerusalem

IN THIS CHAPTER we hear the last of Jerusalem as the headquarters of the Church. The ministry of the gospel is a world-wide ministry. The Church is truly catholic, though, praise God, not Roman Catholic, which in itself is a contradiction in terms. While catholic means "general," Roman is "local," so that Roman Catholic forms the nonsense of local-general. Jerusalem is no longer the center, and there is no warrant whatever for making Rome the center. True worship is universal—neither in Jerusalem nor in Rome nor in any other city; but wherever saints meet together, there the Lord is in the midst.

The Church, in Scripture, knows nothing of any controlling board, of a human head, or any other official set-up. The Lord Himself is the Head of the Church; the Holy Spirit the operating and guiding Power. In chapter 15 we have the last "official" act. As in this chapter we have passed the middle of the book of Acts and are heading for the Epistles to follow, so in this council at Jerusalem we have passed the Jewish touch in Church history and find the gospel henceforth going forth in splendid abandon to the whole world. As Paul said: "Lo, we turn to the Gentiles."

All spiritual ties with Jewish teaching are now broken.

Some Jewish believers had insisted that it was necessary that Gentile believers should be circumcised and be commanded to keep the law of Moses (verse 5). Ah, it was hard for Jews to give up their religion, which had been instituted by God Himself. They were slow to learn that the law had never been given to be kept, but rather to prove that man could *not* keep it, for by the law is the knowledge of sin. They found it hard to learn that circumcision was meant only to prove that, while the literal flesh might be cut off, the flesh spiritually—as evil human nature—is incorrigible, as Paul says in Romans 2:25: "For circumcision verily profiteth, *if thou keep the law*" [which no one ever did]: "but if thou be a breaker of the law, thy circumcision is made uncircumcision." When the grace of God came in to save sinners, then circumcision lost its meaning as a religious rite, as Paul says in Galatians 5:2: "If ye be circumcised, Christ shall profit you nothing. . . . Christ is become of no effect unto you, whosoever of you are justified by the law; ye are fallen from grace."

Circumcision had been a sign between the Lord and the children of Israel. The Lord said in John 7:22 that "Moses gave unto you circumcision," which is confirmed in Leviticus 12:2, where this rite is definitely given to the children of Israel. It has no relation to Gentiles at all, and, as Paul says, even for Jewish believers to do it would be equivalent to going back under the bondage of the law (Galatians 5:3), and to forfeit "the liberty wherewith Christ hath made us free." This is Peter's argument too in this chapter, in full accord with the

Apostle Paul's treatise in Galatians. Peter says: "Now therefore why tempt ye God to put a yoke upon the neck of the disciples, which neither our fathers nor we were able to bear" (verse 10).

Three prominent speakers are heard at this conclave —Peter, Paul, and James. Peter speaks first. Cornelius' conversion, entirely apart from any legal observances, mightily impressed him. As we know, he had to be prepared for it by the vision of the great sheet let down from heaven. He uses it as an effective argument here, and closes his statement with the tender, gracious words, "We believe that through the grace of the Lord Jesus Christ we shall be saved, even as they." He does not say, "They shall be saved, even as we," but brings himself and his own race down to the level of the Gentiles.

By the way, it is interesting to find Peter at this meeting. You remember he fled after his miraculous deliverance from prison, yet here he is back at the same old stand. These mighty men were not easily moved.

Paul follows and gives an account of the mighty work done among the Gentiles, and how God had attested, by many mighty wonders and miracles, that it was His work.

James sums up, and suggests the decision to be delivered to the believers among the Gentiles. He quotes from the Prophet Amos to substantiate his verdict, and here again is one of those remarkable instances in Scripture of the use of what is called the "law of double reference." James cites from Amos 9:11-12, a passage which in reality applies to Israel's future conversion and to the bringing in of the Gentiles in the day of Israel's great tribulation and consequent conversion. The passage actually looks on to a day then far away, but James applies it to the conversion of the Gentiles now—during the day of grace. Amos 9:12 says that Israel "may possess the remnant of *Edom*"; James calls it "the residue of men." The word Edom is the same as Adam and so means "man." Since man in general is in view here, James substitutes that for "Edom," which is a specific nation. James' use of the passage is a beautiful instance of the richness and applicability of God's Word.

James' judgment contains three points: Liberty, for grace delivers the believer from legal Jewish bondage; Purity (verse 20), for they were to keep from pollution, fornication, etc.; Charity, for there was to be liberty of conscience; fellowship was to be on the basis of love, not of light. Paul argues these points at length in 1 Corinthians 8 and Romans 14.

Paul and Barnabas, together with Silas and Judas, carry this verdict, causing great joy among the saints, and the Lord continues to bless His Word among them.

The Second Missionary Journey

ACTS 15:40 TO 18:22

THIS SECOND TRIP is specially noted because the gospel is steadily carried westward, and brought by Paul into Europe for the first time.

The journey begins on a rather sad note, yet God overrules even man's failure for His own interests and glory. Paul and Barnabas part company. The bone of contention is Mark, who had previously proved—in Paul's estimation—unworthy of confidence. Preachers too are human, and do not always agree. As a result of the disagreement the work of the Lord is extended and more souls are reached. We know now that later on Mark was fully restored to Paul's confidence (2 Timothy 4:11), and the once unfaithful servant is chosen of God to write the Gospel about God's perfect Servant—the Lord Jesus Christ.

16

The Gospel in Philippi

ACTS 16

ACCORDING TO the opening verse of this chapter Paul returns to Lystra, where he had been stoned some time before. Here he meets Timothy, who becomes Mark's successor as Paul's traveling companion. Timothy became Paul's closest friend, whom he lovingly speaks of as his "son." Timothy had been carefully instructed by his Jewish mother in the Holy Scriptures (2 Timothy 1:5 and 3:15). Since Timothy's father was a Gentile, the lad had not been circumcised and in order not to offend the Jews needlessly, Paul circumcised Him. There was nothing inconsistent in this, for we must remember that while, as seen in Acts 15, the opinion had been given that circumcision did not apply to the Gentiles, many of the Jewish believers still continued to practise it. People seldom relinquish habits immediately; it takes time.

As they went through the cities, churches were established in the truths of assembly life, and new assemblies were formed through the preaching of the gospel (verse 5). God blessed His Word as Christ was preached.

Paul's original purpose was to revisit the churches in all the cities where he had previously labored (see Acts 15:36), but verses 6 and 7 of our chapter show God had other plans. The Holy Spirit forbade them to preach the Word in Asia and hindered them from going into Bithynia. Paul first went throughout the provinces of Phrygia and Galatia, where later on he spent considerably more time (see Acts 18:23). But the Spirit of God would not let him continue southwestward into Asia, nor northward into Bithynia. Going in a straight westward course and passing by the province of Mysia, Paul came to Troas on the Aegean sea.

Note the "they" in verse 8 and the "we" in verse 10. This means that Luke, the author of the book of Acts, now had joined the missionary band—the first medical missionary on record. Apparently Luke from here on remained steadfastly with the apostle, even sharing the years of trial in Rome, for Paul could write from the Roman prison, "only Luke is with me." What a comfort such a faithful, gifted, and loving friend must have been to Paul, while no doubt Luke looked after the physical well-being of God's great servant.

As Paul was at Troas, looking across the sea toward Europe, there appeared a vision to him, a man of Macedonia praying: "Come over into Macedonia, and help us." Seeing that the way elsewhere had been closed by the Spirit, Paul concluded this invitation must indeed be of God; so the party sailed across, landing at Neapolis and, crossing the mountains, came to Philippi, a Roman colony and the chief city of Macedonia. Philippi was a military base; a miniature Rome, as it were. There does not seem to have been a synagogue there (compare this with Acts 17:1), and so Paul and his friends joined a little group of women on the Sabbath day. These had been in the habit of meeting together for prayer, and Paul used the opportunity to speak of Christ to them.

The Lord opened the heart of a woman named Lydia, who worshiped God but probably never had heard the glorious gospel, as now for the first time it was presented. This woman became Europe's first convert. How precious to read that the Lord opened her heart! We preach and sing to sinners to "open their hearts and let the Saviour in," but the turning of the key that has locked Him out so many years is done by the Lord Himself. A statement like this tells afresh of the sovereignty of God who awakens sinners to a sense of their need. Lydia proves her faith immediately by her confession of Him in baptism, and then by extending hospitality to the servants of God. Lydia, like the Ethiopian eunuch, Cornelius, or Paul himself, was anything but what the world would call a sinner, but she nevertheless needed a Saviour. Later on in this chapter we have the conversion of a hard, brutal prison warden. Good people and bad people—all alike need the saving grace of God. Lydia's household was also saved, as was that of the jailor later.

When the Lord works, the devil too gets busy. A demon-possessed poor woman for many days trailed the servants of God, commending them as true ministers of the way of salvation. But the devil's commendation is less to be desired than his condemnation, so Paul rebukes her and tells the evil spirit to come out of her. Then Satan shows his true colors; the apostles are hauled before the magistrates and without any investigation being instituted, they are beaten and thrown into a dungeon. (Their experience in the prison and the conversion of the jailor we shall look at in a special article later on.)

For some unexplained reason (perhaps the magistrates had realized how flagrantly they had violated all rules of Roman judicial procedure) the next morning the magistrates sent an order for the release of the prisoners (Acts 16:35-40). But Paul replies: "They have beaten us openly uncondemned, being Romans, and have cast us into prison; and now do they thrust us out privily? nay verily, but let them come themselves and fetch us out."

Hearing they were Romans, the magistrates were filled with fear and came and besought them to please leave the city. I believe one has a right to deduce that Paul and Silas forcefully told those officials about their unjust and wicked treatment. Though a believer may suffer for Christ's sake, he is nevertheless a citizen of his country, and has a right to expect proper consideration of his rights as a citizen. Today probably some would sue the city for unlawful imprisonment and abuse and collect a good sum in damages.

It is to be noted that Paul did not tell them they were Romans the night before, when he could have avoided the brutal treatment they suffered. He was not seeking to escape suffering for Christ when he protested to these magistrates. The result of his forbearance was that they proved the presence of God with them in the remarkable incident of the night, and saw His blessing in the salvation of the jailor (which, by the way, has been the cause of the salvation of thousands since). As a result, too, a thriving assembly was formed in Philippi. How sweet to read in verse 40 that Paul and Silas *comforted* the brethen and departed. One would have thought that they themselves needed comfort.

17

Paul at Thessalonica

ACTS 17:1-9

PASSING THROUGH the cities of Amphipolis and Apollonia (nothing is said of Paul's labors in either place) the messengers of Christ came to Thessalonica, about one hundred miles southwest of Philippi; and fifty miles further along the same road they later came to Berea. Here there was a synagogue into which Paul entered and for three Sabbath days reasoned with them out of the Scriptures, proving from them that Christ must have suffered, died, and risen again from the dead, and then proving that Jesus of Nazareth was the Christ (verse 3). Of the Jews only a few believed, but a vast multitude from the Gentiles did so, including many women of prominence in that city. As usual, this aroused the envy and hatred of the unbelieving Jews, who assaulted the house where Paul was a guest. When they could not find him, they drew Paul's host, Jason, before the rulers of the city, saying: "These men who have turned the world upside down are come hither also." This charge was unique, was it not? The truth is, though, that the world is upside down as it is; if men would only obey the gospel, the world would then be turned right side up again.

The brethren sent Paul and Silas by night to the next city—Berea. Again, they immediately enter the syna-

gogue and preach Christ. What a splendid thing is said
of the Bereans in verse 11: "These were more noble than
those of Thessalonica, in that they received the word
with all readiness of mind, and searched the scriptures
daily, whether those things were so." They did not take
even the apostle's word for it, but compared for themselves what he said with the written Word. Would to
God all Christians were willing to do so! No wonder
that many believed.

From fifty miles away revengeful Jews come down
to Berea to stir up opposition. Paul is sent away to
Athens, while Silas and Timothy remain at Berea. One
seems to see here the tender consideration these friends
had for God's dear servant. They do not want him ex-
posed to any possible chance of harm or death. They
consider themselves unimportant and are content to remain and face whatever danger might lurk in the trouble
stirred up by these Thessalonian Jews. Paul in the meantime sails three hundred miles southward to Athens, and
there waits for Timothy and Silas to rejoin him.

Paul at Athens

ACTS 17:16-34

ATHENS WAS the acknowledged center of intellect, culture, and religion. It was the seat of the prevailing schools

of philosophy, but it was "wholly given to idolatry" (verse 16). Naturally so, for philosophy and religion revolve around "self," and to make self the center is the essence of idolatry. It was said there were more gods than men in Athens. And it is no different in our day. Almost the whole human race is bowing down before idols which human minds have invented and human hands have made. Some worship crude idols of wood and stone or bow down before pictures and images; others are not so crude, but worship the gods of gold and silver, of culture and refinement, of arts and sciences, etc., etc.— everything but the worship of the true God.

At Athens there were two main schools of philosophy —of the Epicureans and of the Stoics. They may not be called by these names now, but the same philosophies thrive today.

The Epicureans were materialists and atheists mostly. They taught that the chief aim of existence is pleasure; that pleasure is the only good and pain the only evil. To them there was no God and therefore no future life or retribution: "Let us eat and drink for tomorrow we die." Needless to say there are untold millions of Epicureans today who never even heard of that ancient society. Men are still lovers of pleasure more than lovers of God. Such live in a fool's paradise, making themselves believe that since they do not believe there is a God or a hereafter, therefore there is none. And millions more, who nominally believe in a God, live daily as if God did not exist.

The Stoics taught that God was everything and in

everything, which is called Pantheism. A modern-day imitation of it is known as Christian Science. Stoics were fatalists and considered apathy the highest moral attainment. God with them was the "soul" of the universe, so that the distinction between the human and the divine ceased to exist. Man became his own god. This is the basic teaching of all spiritistic cults, with infinite variations of course, as in Christian Science, Unity, Spiritualism, etc.

To such philosophers Christian truth, which is so simple, so matter of fact, was absurd. They considered Paul a babbler, talking baby talk. Speaking to these men of God, in His relation to the world and to men, Paul declares Him to be the Creator and the world's moral Governor; truths which strike at the very heart of materialism, pantheism, atheism, and every other "ism." Paul spoke to them of sin as a personal offense against a personal God and Judge, who therefore commands all men everywhere to repent. He shows the folly of idolatry when we ourselves are the offspring of God and therefore greater in worth than all other created beings or things. He warns them of the judgment to come at the hands of that Man "whom God has ordained, and whereof He has given assurance unto all men in that He has raised Him from the dead." Paul never failed to call attention to this radical and revolutionary truth of the resurrection of Christ. No doubt much more was said by Paul on this occasion, but the Spirit of God has recorded only the main theme.

God has hid these things from the wise and prudent

and has revealed them unto babes, and the result of Paul's message to these intelligentsia confirms this axiom. Only a few believed; most of them mocked. The gospel produces the usual threefold result: some believe; many reject it; some procrastinate.

18

Paul at Corinth

ACTS 18:1-22

WHEN PAUL WENT to Athens he had urged Timothy and Silas to join him there as soon as possible (Acts 17:15), but they never did so. Not till Paul had left Athens and had come to Corinth did these two finally meet him again (18:5).

This Corinth comes to occupy quite a place in the New Testament canon of Scripture. It was a very wicked, licentious city, but was chosen of God to furnish the setting for the ministry in regard to church organization, fellowship, worship, etc., as well as to supply all needed guidance for all matters pertaining to the gathering of believers and their testimony for the Lord, as of those who gather to the Name of the Lord Jesus Christ. The two Epistles to the Corinthians provide all the teaching necessary for Christian life, conduct, and ministry; they are the divine charter for the Church as a witness for Christ.

At Corinth Paul met Aquila and Priscilla, a godly couple who became some of Paul's dearest friends and helpers. For the first time we read of Paul working with his hands. He explains later on, in writing to the Corinthians, that he did so in order to rob them of any opportunity to say that he was in the business of preaching the gospel for the sake of financial advantage (see 2 Corinthians 11:7-12).

As a result of his faithful ministry at Corinth, in spite of much opposition, many of the Corinthians hearing, believed and were baptized (verse 8), giving us the scriptural order in the salvation and consecration of the soul. The Lord assured Paul in a vision of His protecting care, and Paul continued there a year and six months, teaching the Word of God among them.

The opposing Jews bring Paul before Gallio, the Roman deputy, but he refuses to judge in religious matters; when they beat Sosthenes, a ruler of the synagogue, we read that "Gallio cared for none of those things." Others have said that this did not suggest religious indifference on the part of Gallio, but rather religious tolerance. Gallio was the brother of Seneca, the famed philosopher, and was known as "sweet Gallio." He was a man of a most attractive character, just and upright; and so he felt that no man should be tried as a criminal because of his religious beliefs. He represents the proper attitude for a politician—the separation of church and state.

It is sad indeed that professing Christians through the centuries have been guilty of seeking the destruction of those who disagree with them on spiritual matters. God's Word does not condone in any wise persecution for the sake of matters of the heart and conscience. "Vengeance is Mine, I will repay, saith the Lord."

After staying yet a long while in Corinth, Paul leaves, taking his new-found friends, Aquila and Priscilla, with

him, and comes to the city of Ephesus. He had shorn his
head in Cenchrea, having made a vow, but we do not
know what the vow was about. He remains in Ephesus
only briefly, but promises to return, which he did later,
when he stayed for three years. The removal of Aquila
and Priscilla to Ephesus, and probably the favorable im-
pressions received by Paul during this stop-off, opened
the way for his subsequent long visit on his third missionary journey (see Acts 20:31). Thus ends the second missionary journey, as Paul returns to Antioch,
whence he set forth (verse 22).

The Third Missionary Journey

ACTS 18:23 TO 21:16

THE MAIN FEATURE of this third pioneer evangelistic
tour was Paul's three years of labor in Ephesus. His ministry is set off by two incidents: one before, the other
after Paul's arrival at Ephesus. These two things empha-
size the fullness of the gospel of Christ which Paul elsewhere calls "my" gospel. In contrast we see how
Apollos preached the elementary truth of repentance,
knowing only the baptism of John (18:25); while the
disciples of John had been saved by receiving John's
message of repentance, and accordingly they had been

baptized with John's baptism. Aquila and Princilla set Apollos straight. He must have been a humble soul, for, though a powerful, eloquent preacher, he allowed two common, poor tentmakers to instruct him in the things of God "more perfectly."

As Apollos was disposed to go to Corinth, the saints at Ephesus commended him, exhorting the brethen elsewhere to receive him (verse 27). This commendation was not for reception into Christian fellowship, which was then freely extended to all true believers and should be done so now, but it was for reception as a minister of the Word. Preachers permitted on Christian platforms should be known as scripturally sound and reliable, or, if unknown, should be commended by responsible brethren. Paul speaks of this in 2 Corinthians 3:1. He was there certainly not referring to reception at the Lord's Table, but to commendation as a servant of Christ. He personally did not need such, for they themselves were the fruit of his labors; they were his epistle of commendation.

19

Paul at Ephesus

ACTS 19

THE INCIDENT in the first seven verses of this chapter shows that the baptism of John was now obsolete, and that the proper baptism is Christian baptism. John baptized *unto* the remission of sins; Christian baptism is consequent to the remission of sins. Paul baptized these anew, setting aside John's baptism as irrelevant. Paul baptized them; and then, by the laying on of his hands, the Holy Ghost came upon these disciples and they spoke with tongues. The whole is somewhat similar to what happened at Pentecost, and so these verses have been called the Ephesian Pentecost.

This same application might be made as to the entire chapter 19 of Acts. As at Pentecost, there is not only the outpouring of the Holy Spirit and the speaking with tongues, but also the bold testimony borne to the Jews; the rejection of the gospel by many; the reception of it by the multitudes (see verse 20); lives transformed by the power of the Spirit (verses 17-19); and the accompaniment of miracles (verses 11-12). All these have an analogy to the days of Pentecost. Thus God worked mightily in this Asian capital as He did in the Jewish capital in Acts 2. As the Church is composed of Jew and Gentile united into one Body by the Cross, Acts 2 presents the story of the Jewish work; Acts 19 the Gentile.

Chapter 19 closes by showing that the very institution of idolatry seems to be tottering under the mighty impact of the gospel of Christ. Indeed, wherever Christ is received Judaism as well as heathenism receives staggering blows.

How striking to read that this Demetrius pretends a concern for the goddess Diana and her religion, yet is honest enough to confess he is thinking of his own interests. This new doctrine preached by Paul strikes at his pocketbook. He is concerned with personal gain while Paul, the Christian, labors at great cost to himself (see Philippians 3:7) for the gain of others only. Those saved by the grace of God not only do not seek personal gain, but surrender their wealth (they made a bonfire at a cost of about 50,000 pieces of silver), having become the possessors of the unsearchable riches of Christ. Self-seeking and self-centered is the natural man; self-surrendering and seeking the blessing of others is the follower of Christ. Idolatry has no message, but can shout for two hours at the top of its voice to make itself believe that that is true which is not true. Unbelief still can scream and shout and rant, but can say nothing constructive or informative. It is interesting to see God's little "assembly" pitted against the whole "assembly" (verse 41) of the city of Ephesus. God's Church has won for it still stands today, but Diana of the Ephesians has long since vanished. Great may be any philosophy, religion, or idolatry, but "Greater" is He whose Name we adore, and who shall yet hold universal sway.

20

Macedonia, Greece, Troas, and Miletus

ACTS 20:1-16

PAUL REVISITED Macedonia, then went to Greece, where
he stayed for three months (verse 3). The first two
verses of this chapter dispense with the visit to Macedonia, but Paul's second Epistle to the Corinthians throws
clear light upon his purpose and the trials through which
he passed while there. That letter was written in Macedonia on his way to Greece (2 Corinthians 1:16; 2:13).
As the Jews laid wait to kill Paul (Acts 20:3), he gave
up the thought of returning directly to Antioch and
went in the opposite direction to Macedonia. He again
visited Philippi and sailed from there across the Aegean
sea to Troas.

The incident of the young man falling out of the window—recorded in verses 7-12—is full of instruction and
is treated later in detail. So also Paul's farewell address to
the elders at Ephesus is considered at length later in this
book.

No other paragraph in the New Testament contains
more direct, practical advice for missionaries and all
Christian workers than Paul's address in this chapter.
Looking back (verses 19-21), Paul speaks of his lowli-
ness of mind, his patience under trials, his faithfulness in
the ministry of Christ to all classes and in all places—

both public and private. Referring to the present, he declares it is his duty to go to Jerusalem, in spite of the afflictions that await him there. As to the future, he is sure that his work in Ephesus is ended and so he exhorts the elders to be faithful as overseers of the flock of God. In verses 33-35 he cites his own example as a guide for them, as he labored wholly for the blessing of others, seeking nothing for himself. The whole address gives us a holy insight into the heart of the great apostle of the Gentiles. No wonder they wept and kissed him as they saw his face for the last time—to see him again only in the glory above.

21

Paul's Journey to Jerusalem

ACTS 21:1-16

PAUL AND his co-workers leave Miletus and without interruption go on to Tyre. After a seven-day stay there, they proceed to Caesarea. At Tyre too there is a sad farewell taken of God's honored servant. At Caesarea once more with tears the saints urge him not to go on to Jerusalem, but all their pleading is in vain. Two features stand out in all this: the deep affection in which Paul is held by his friends and fellow saints and servants, and his determination to face the trials that await him. Both in Tyre and in Caesarea Paul is urged not to go further. Did he do right in ignoring those pleas? Acts 21:14 seems to show the saints felt he had the will of the Lord in the path he took; who are we to judge otherwise?

Thus ends Paul's third missionary journey. The fourth—to Rome—was a forced one, but no doubt used of God for rich blessing to many.

Helpful Hints on Missionary Work
Gleaned from Paul's Experiences
During His First Three Journeys

I understand some sixteen years had elapsed—at the opening of chapter 13—since Paul had received his commission, at his conversion, to carry to the Gentiles the gospel of the grace of God. (Acts 9:15). Paul was called to be a "foreign" missionary to the regions beyond, and Antioch became the center whence his ministry radiated. His experiences illustrate missionary methods and principles that are as valid and vital today. The three opening verses of chapter 13 tell us that missionary enterprise demands that the church at home be spiritual, prayerful, self-denying, taught in the Word, and concerned about the work of the Lord at home and abroad.

The missionaries themselves were men strong spiritually and very likely also physically, called to the work by the Holy Spirit. This call was recognized to be of God by the local church, which set its stamp of approval on that call by the laying of hands of the saints on the missionaries, thus expressing their fellowship with them. It is never wise for servants of Christ to go forth in full-time service, or to any special field, unless in complete harmony with the Christians with whom they are associated. It is hardly necessary to say that Acts 13:1-3 does not teach human ordination to the ministry, for Saul (later called Paul) had been preaching for years before this and tells us himself that he was an apostle not of men, neither by man, but by Jesus Christ and God the Father (Galatians 1:1).

Opposition beset these servants almost immediately (Acts 13:6-12); that, and violent persecution dogged them all along the road, but God worked mightily. The messengers of the cross may expect to meet bitter antagonism, but God's Word does not return to Him void.

The course of Paul at Iconium stresses two points in missionary strategy: (1) Paul sought to reach all classes and races; (2) he usually went to the larger centers of population and there, by the preaching of the gospel, formed churches from which the Word would radiate to outlying districts.

We read that Paul and Barnabas fled from Iconium to Derbe and Lystra (Acts 14:6). The question is: is that what missionaries should do in times of danger? I believe this would depend on circumstances and the felt guidance of the Spirit. The Lord Jesus Himself frequently withdrew and hid Himself, certainly not from fear, but no doubt with a wise purpose in view. Paul returned to these places later on, probably when the agitation had died down and there was a more ready ear for the message.

At Lystra Paul preached differently than he did at Antioch in Pisidia, where his message was as recorded in Acts 13. There he preached to Jews; in chapter 14 to Gentiles, who were practically heathen. To the Jews in chapter 13 he quotes Scripture, for they knew the Scriptures; to the others he speaks of God as the One whose power and love are seen in the works of Nature and Providence. In view of the goodness of such a living and loving God he called on his hearers to repent. Even so every wise missionary suits his message to his audience; and of course every wise servant in the home field does likewise.

In chapter 15 we see that the problems which brought Paul and Barnabas up to Jerusalem were caused by missionary activities. Missionaries are always creating problems. Their work demands men and money, thought and prayer; their needs call for cooperation among the saints —saints of all types and opinions. The main issue was then: "What is the right missionary message?" The missionary's work is not found in the social realm, except as an aid to reach souls with the message of life eternal. The message should be the clear-cut truth of man's lost, guilty condition, and the glorious news of the forgiveness of sins through faith in Christ; with this leading to a life of holiness and service—all this through faith in Christ, without any qualifying additions. Paul preached this, but others introduced the idea that circumcision and the keeping of the law of Moses were also necessary. The verdict of this council at Jerusalem was that the break with Judaism was complete and absolute—no circumcision or keeping of the law, but spiritual liberty. But note that baptism was not abrogated. Circumcision was Jewish; baptism is Christian.

The contention between Paul and Barnabas (Acts 15: 36-41) is a sad proof that missionaries too are human and so do not always agree. In such cases it is better to agree to disagree, as long as grudges are not held and animosity is not engendered. Many such instances have happened during the history of missionary enterprise, but as long as the work is carried forward in the spirit of humility, God can and will overrule all for the furtherance of the gospel, as in this case. The work went on in two directions at the same time, as Paul goes with Silas, and Barnabas and Mark sail for Cyprus.

In Acts 16: 10 we find that Luke, the beloved physician and author of this history of the early church, joins the party. He is the pioneer in that loyal army of medical missionaries who have cared for the bodies as well as souls of many around the world.

The account of Lydia suggests, in her entertainment of the apostle, the invaluable support given by sisters in Christ to the cause of Christ throughout the ages. How much most of us owe to them God only knows, and He will reward them richly. Paul did not forget them either (Philippians 4:3, etc.). Hospitality to God's servants is one of the bright jewels of Christian grace.

Paul's stay in Thessalonica tells the story of how the gospel was *preached* (not omitting the precious and challenging truth of the Coming of the Lord for His saints nor the warning of His Coming again to judge the world, as written in 1 Thessalonians 4 and 5). His stay in Berea tells how the gospel should be *received* (with all readiness of mind, searching the Scriptures, whether these things are so). The book of Acts and the Epistles to the Thessalonians lay great stress on Paul's type of preaching. It was essentially an exposition of the Scriptures, which still is the most valuable and most needed method of preaching today. Even in instructed Christian circles the lack of understanding and knowledge of God's Word is often rather alarming. There is much preaching on texts, or on some words strung together on a string after the fashion of a necklace; but altogether too little consecutive exposition of the Word itself in its context.

The experiences through which Paul passed at Corinth are described in his second Epistle to the Corinthians. The causes of his discouragement there are common to all the servants of Christ. Look at some of them:

1. Paul felt his loneliness. He looked eagerly for the return of Silas and Timothy, but in the meantime in that great heathen city there was not a friend to whom he could turn for sympathy and companionship. How often have missionaries been weighed down by isolation and separation from friends and loved ones!

2. He suffered because of the lack of funds. (How many of the Lord's servants could recite graphic examples in their own experience!) He went to work at his trade of tentmaker to secure means of livelihood. He was not ashamed to work with his hands and sometimes preachers may have to resort to that; in fact, in many cases it would be best to earn largely one's own living and serve the Lord in spare time. Many areas in this country of ours would benefit greatly if capable young men would settle in some central location and minister the Word in nearby halls or schools, while earning their own living. At least, the proper path for the servant of Christ is to start at home, as the Lord so frequently commanded; then to go further afield if the Lord leads clearly that way.

3. The antagonism of the enemy was specially strong in Corinth (Acts 18:6), and largely by Paul's own countrymen. Today also so often persecution is strongest

from nominal Christians, and this is the hardest to bear.

4. The character of the city where Paul then was—Corinth. It was a prominent city and noted for its extreme immorality; proverbial for its pride, vileness, and idolatry. It was not an easy place to work.

Paul found relief from these oppressing features in many ways, which parallel modern Christian life:

1. He formed new friendships. He became acquainted with a lovely Christian couple—Aquila and Priscilla, who thenceforth assumed a large place in Paul's affection.

2. The daily routine of tentmaking was itself a relief from anxiety and from the heavy mental strain placed on him by the mighty, complex truths revealed to Paul and which he preached and wrote. Manual labor furnishes gratifying relaxation from mental stress, as this writer happens to know very well.

3. The preaching every Sabbath gave him deep joy, as he spoke of the Saviour so precious to him.

4. The arrival of Silas and Timothy, with gifts from Macedonia (see Philippians 4:15) was very cheering and encouraging. Paul appreciated even more than the gifts themselves the spiritual growth and love for him which these gifts expressed.

5. No doubt the supreme joy was a fresh vision of Christ (Acts 18:9-10): "Then spake the Lord to Paul in the night by a vision, Be not afraid, but speak, and hold not thy peace: For I am with thee, and no man shall set on thee to hurt thee: for I have much people in this city." How gracious of the Lord to come in in times of distress with a special message of encouragement. Paul was as-

sured of the presence, the power, and the purpose of the Lord. Here the most prominent church of the New Testament was formed; from here the apostle wrote his great letters to the Thessalonian saints. Trial became the occasion for triumph. It is always so.

Next Paul came to Ephesus, where he stayed at least three years, longer than anywhere else. Possibly because so many years of strenuous and suffering service for Christ were behind him, and his age would naturally slow him down, he now stayed longer in any given place. As servants of Christ increase in age and it becomes more difficult for them to travel, their usefulness to the saints is often increased as they are able to minister longer in one place and thus can instruct the saints in the great truths we hold dear and which so much need to be taught. God's people need to be established in the Word. We can learn this lesson from Paul's long visits at Corinth and at Ephesus; after the gospel has been preached and souls have been saved, it is of great importance to care for these newborn souls, to establish them in God's truth, and to see them gathered in Christian fellowship. Paul speaks of this twofold ministry in Ephesians 3:8-9: "to preach . . . the unsearchable riches of Christ" [that is, to preach the gospel to sinners]; and then "to make all men see what is the fellowship of the mystery" [that is, to teach the truths concerning the Church and its place on earth as a testimony to Christ].

Acts briefly introduces Apollos, apparently a humble man. A missionary should above all things be humble; willing to sit as well as stand; to be taught as well as teach.

Paul's Arrest

THE REST of the book of Acts is concerned with Paul's experiences as a prisoner of the Lord in the hands of the Romans. The period between his arrest and his release in Rome is reckoned at about five years. The circumstances surrounding his arrest are an epitome, as it were, of those five years: he is a prisoner unjustly confined, protected by Rome from the murderous hatred of the Jews. These two features run throughout the rest of this book.

One cannot help but wonder whether Paul did wrong in taking part with the four men who had a vow (verse 23), specially as by so doing he was to prove to the Jews at Jerusalem that he "himself walked orderly and kept the law" (verse 24). Somehow this seems to militate against the apostle's strong ministry elsewhere in regard to the believers not being under the law, but under grace. Certain it is that the scheme failed and led to his arrest. But we do know that if it was failure on Paul's part, God overruled it for His own glory, as He does any failure of His people.

Rescued out of the hands of the wild mob by the Roman captain, Paul begs leave to speak to his nation and is granted permission (verses 31-40). After a great silence descends on the multitude he speaks to them in the Hebrew tongue.

22

Paul's Five Defenses

ACTS 22 TO 26

ONE BLESSED RESULT of Paul's imprisonment was his opportunity five times over to present Christ to audiences of ever-increasing importance. First (in chapter 22) he speaks to Israel as a nation, represented by the crowd that heard him there; secondly, before the Jewish Sanhedrin, the outstanding religious leaders of the Jewish people (chapter 23); thirdly, before Felix, the Roman governor (chapter 24); fourthly, before Governor Festus (chapter 25), and fifthly, before King Agrippa. From the common people on up, ever higher, till he stands before a king. Thus God overrules the malice of man for the furtherance of His own all-wise purposes.

Paul's Address to the Nation

ACTS 22

PAUL'S MESSAGE here is composed of three chief points:

1. His past (verses 3-5). He was a Jew, of the straightest sect, highly educated, zealous of the law; a fiery zealot and a persecutor of the followers of the hated

Jesus. Hence, if now he is different, some mighty supernatural influence must have come into his life, which he goes on to describe in detail.

2. The present. The power that transformed him from a persecutor to a preacher of this doctrine was a vision of Jesus of Nazareth in the glory (verses 6-16). It is this which accounts for his present convictions.

Two slight differences may be observed between Paul's account here and that in Acts 9, when his conversion actually took place. Here Paul says that it was Jesus "of Nazareth" who spoke to him from the glory, which words are omitted in Acts 9. No doubt they were spoken by the Lord and Paul cites them here, for he would have the Jews know that it is the very Nazarene, by them rejected and despised, who is indeed their Messiah.

So also in Acts 9 it states that those with Paul heard a voice, while here it says "they heard *not* the voice of Him that spake to me" (verse 9). The explanation is that in chapter 9 they heard "a" voice; here they heard not "the" voice of Him. They heard a sound but not the words spoken. Even so millions still hear the sound of the gospel, but do not get the message. To Paul alone the sound of the voice conveyed an intelligent message. In our chapter we learn not only that Paul heard the voice of Jesus, but that he saw Him as well (verse 14). Spiritually interpreted, that is how every sinner is saved. He hears the voice of the Son of God in the gospel message (John 5:25) and by faith sees Jesus as his Saviour (Hebrews 2:9).

To the fact of his baptism at Ananias' hands Paul adds
here that he was told to "arise . . . and wash away thy
sins" (verse 16). How much capital men have made of
this command, as though sins are washed away by the
water of baptism. Since when does man cleanse *himself*
from his sins, and where in Scripture is water shown to
have the power to remove the stain of sin? God's Word
plainly says that it is "the blood of Jesus Christ that
cleanseth from all sin." If it cleanseth from "all" sin,
where is any sin left for water to wash away? The simple truth is that in baptism the believer washes away his
sins in the sight of men, while blood does it before God.
In baptism one takes the stand that he is buried with
Christ and thus is through with sin; that henceforth he
will not serve sin. He washes away—in the sight of
others—the filth that once marked him. Blood meets the
guilt of sin before God; baptism the *filth* of sin before
men. In baptism, in picture, one puts off the old man and
puts on the new, as Galatians 3:27 tells us: "As many of
you as have been baptized into Christ have put on
Christ."

3. The future. Paul received a call from his newfound
Saviour and Lord to get out of Jerusalem and to go far
hence unto the Gentiles. And once more—as at Pentecost and as at Stephen's death—the nation persists in its
rejection of God's mercy. Perhaps some twenty-five
years have passed since Peter preached Christ on the day
of Pentecost, but Israel has not revised its attitude towards Christ; it is still "We will not have this Man to
reign over us."

23

Paul's Address Before the Jewish Supreme Council

ACTS 23

PAUL IS rescued the second time by the centurion and his soldiers, and the next day is brought before the Sanhedrin. Scripture tells us very little of what was said on this occasion; eternity will tell the results. One loves to think that some of those who listened may have had their consciences reached and their hearts turned to the Messiah who came to redeem them.

Once again Paul is saved out of their hands by the power of Rome. It is truly ironical that Paul's own people sought his destruction, while the enemies of Israel protected him. What a commentary on Israel's moral depravity! Life and justice were more secure in the hands of a heathen government than under the degenerate rule of the professing people of God.

Paul's opening word before the Sanhedrin is of note: "I have lived in all good conscience before God until this day." Paul was never a hypocrite or a timeserver. Even when he was murdering Christians his conscience was clear. It only shows what a wretched guide one's conscience can be. Someone has said that a conscience is like a wheelbarrow: you push it where you want it to go. A conscience must be enlightened by God's truth before it can be reliable. The conscience of the sinner is evil

154

(Hebrews 10:2), and needs to be purged by the blood of Christ (Hebrews 9:14).

The rest of Acts 23 is concerned with elaborate precautions taken by Lysias, the Roman captain, to assure Paul's safe delivery to the Roman governor Felix. More than forty men had sworn an oath that they would neither eat nor drink till they had killed Paul (verse 21). I imagine that is one vow they broke.

Captain Lysias' letter to governor Felix is a typical example of smooth politics. He had bound Paul uncondemned and would have scourged him if Paul had not spoken out (22:25). To make sure this flagrant offense against Roman law would not get him into trouble, he cleverly garbles the truth by pretending that he rescued Paul out of the people's hands because he knew that Paul was a Roman—which was a downright lie. However, if it should come out that he had bound Paul, it would be his word against this poor prisoner's; so Lysias forestalled any possible unpleasantness after this fashion. Apart from that, he seems to have been kind in his treatment of Paul and in dealing with Paul's nephew (Acts 23:16-22).

24

Paul Before Felix

ACTS 24

HISTORY TELLS us that Felix was noted for his profligate personal life and his cruelty in his capacity as a Roman official. Before him Paul now answers for himself in reply to the accusations brought against him by the high priest and the elders of the Jews, with a certain orator named Tertullus as the spokesman. His name, meaning *triple-hardened*, may well typify Israel's condition, triple-hardened as they were, as we mentioned in the previous chapter. After the usual diplomatic and political wordiness about the nobility of the ignoble Felix (the Jews hated him like poison), Tertullus charges the apostle with guilt under three indictments:

1. Paul was guilty of sedition, for he was a "mover of sedition among all the Jews throughout the world." This is put first and probably stressed, for it would make Paul culpable, and guilty of death under Roman law. Paul answers this ridiculous charge by saying he had made no speeches, had gathered no crowd; in short, he had been there only a few days and the charge was utterly false (verses 11-13).

2. He was charged with heresy in that he was the ringleader of the sect of the Nazarenes. Verses 14-16

contain his noble reply to this accusation as he says: "But this I confess unto thee, that after the way which they call heresy, so worship I the God of my fathers, believing all things which are written in the law and in the prophets: and have hope toward God, which they themselves also allow, that there shall be a resurrection of the dead, both of the just and unjust. And herein do I exercise myself, to have always a conscience void of offense toward God, and toward men."

A few thoughts here are worthy of special note.

Paul ignores the name of "Nazarene" which is put upon him. The only name he recognizes is the precious Name of Jesus Christ. Christianity sets aside all other names to acknowledge only the Name which God has put above every other name.

Paul speaks of two resurrections—of the just and of the unjust. In the Old Testament only one general resurrection is taught, but the New Testament unveils the truth that there are two main resurrections, separated by at least one thousand years (Revelation 20:4-6). Under grace there is a separation between the saved and the lost; not only hereafter, but right now as well. Perhaps this was one of the chief causes for the Jews' hatred and envy, for those who were truly the Lord's, saved by His grace, were separating themselves from the nation of Israel. Grace was calling Christ's true sheep out from the Jewish sheepfold (see John 10:1-4), bringing into sharp relief the fact that the others were only false, empty professors. Satan hates nothing more than he hates separation to Christ. Hereafter, believers shall be raised from the dead at Christ's Coming for His own, as seen in 1 Thessalonians 4:13-18; sinners not till a thousand years later.

3. The third charge was that of sacrilege—profaning the temple. Paul nullifies this by stating that, instead of profaning the temple, he had come to Jerusalem to bring relief to his nation and, while engaged in the most sacred rites, was falsely accused and arrested.

The question might be raised here—why does Paul answer these false charges when our blessed Lord, before Pilate, refused to say anything when so accused? I believe that Jesus did not refute false accusations because He had come to bear our sin and guilt. As far as man's part went, our Lord went to the cross unjustly. He was numbered with transgressors, but unjustly. Paul, on the contrary, was not a prisoner to suffer judgment for sin that was not his own; hence he bore witness to the truth and to the falsity of the lies uttered.

Felix, consistent with the habit of judges everywhere, puts off his judgment till later. He had the fond hope that perhaps this valuable prisoner might fill his greedy hands with a bribe; but this proved a vain hope. Yet Paul's defense must have impressed him, for after a while he, with his wife Drusilla, sent for him and heard him concerning the faith in Christ. His famous prisoner spoke to him in no uncertain tones concerning righteousness, temperance, and judgment to come, a threefold message hitting the center of the target, for Felix was known for his unrighteous rule, his utter lack of temperance (self-control) in his personal life, which might well lead him to fear the judgment to come. Paul fearlessly touched upon all these sore spots and Felix trembled as he listened to him.

Though Felix would not bow to the truth, yet it had a mesmeric charm for him, for he sent for Paul often and talked with him. But, since he left the apostle a prisoner for two years and still left him so when his successor Festus took office, there is strong reason to doubt that Felix ever turned in repentance to Christ. Can you imagine a man listening again and again—in private conversation—to a preacher so earnest and so gifted as the apostle Paul, and yet die without Christ? He hoped for money to "loose" Paul (verse 26), but he himself remained unloosed from the slavery of sin and passion; he was far more "bound" than his prisoner was. He put off things to a "convenient" season, as do so many still, failing to realize that *now* is the convenient season; *today* is the day of salvation. He left Paul bound.

One wonders what Paul did during those two years. Perhaps study the Word a great deal, and gather thoughts later on in Rome to be put into writing, giving us the great New Testament spiritual Epistles. God's weary servant got some much needed quiet and rest.

25

Paul Before Festus

ACTS 25

ACCORDING TO profane history Porcius Festus was a man of much higher character than Felix. But he too, instead of dispensing justice, seeks to please men when he asks Paul whether he would go to Jerusalem, there to be judged of the things wherewith he is charged. Paul appeals unto Caesar. I certainly will not be a judge of whether the apostle did wrong in committing himself to the emperor's judgment. We do know that the Lord stood by him after his defense before the Jewish Sanhedrin and comforted him with the words: "Be of good cheer, Paul, for as thou hast testified of Me in Jerusalem, so must thou bear witness also at Rome" (23:11). What stands out here, as all through the book of Acts, is the continued and unchanging attitude of the nation of Israel in rejecting the gospel of God's grace.

Although two years have elapsed since Paul's arrest, the Jews are still laying in wait to kill him (25:3). The same old charges are preferred, as before Felix (verses 7-8), as is evident from Paul's defense in verse 8; this one verse covers Paul's answer given in more detail in his answer before Felix. Paul was probably getting weary of the impasse that had kept him a prisoner in Caesarea when he was anxious to get to Rome; perhaps the Spirit definitely guided him to make this move. At any rate, he appeals to Caesar.

After certain days King Agrippa and Bernice came to Caesarea to see Festus; and Festus, after some time, declares Paul's cause to this profligate son of the wicked Herod who slew James, the brother of John, with the sword, and who sought to do the same to Peter, as recorded in Acts 12.

Festus, in apprising King Agrippa of Paul's case, says that he told Paul's accusers that "It is not the manner of the Romans to deliver any man to die, before that he which is accused have the accusers face to face, and have license to answer for himself concerning the crime laid against him" (verse 16). Festus conveniently forgot that neither was it the custom of the Romans to hold a man prisoner when not a single charge laid against him had been substantiated, as we read in verse 7. As Agrippa suggests later: "This man might have been set at liberty, if he had not appealed unto Caesar" (26:32). But such is politics—then and now as well.

Agrippa expresses a desire to hear Paul, and thus the way is opened for Paul's defense before the highest authority he had yet faced; to go higher yet when he eventually faced the emperor in Rome. Paul's address before the king, as recorded in the next chapter, is one of the most majestic utterances in all the Word of God.

26

Paul's Apology Before Agrippa

ACTS 26

PAUL'S ADDRESS here is of immense value as a defense of the Christian faith; as a statement of its relation to Judaism; and as an exhibition of its character as a message for the whole world. Paul insists that the resurrection of the Lord Jesus is the very heart of Christianity (see verse 23); and that resurrection is not inconsistent with the truth revealed in the Old Testament, for this hope was a promise made of God unto the fathers (verse 6); and thus that God should raise the dead was not at all incredible (verse 8).

One of the differences essential to Christianity was the fact that Christ should be the "first" to rise from the dead (verse 23), but even that, says Paul, was foretold by Moses and the prophets (verses 22-23). Furthermore, he himself had seen this risen, glorified Saviour at God's right hand in Heaven, and thus he could not be disobedient to the heavenly vision (verse 19). Many others had seen the risen Christ upon earth, as he declares in 1 Corinthians 15. But the thing that particularly inflamed the hatred of the Jews was Paul's insistence that Gentiles too could be saved through faith in Christ, and that the Jews also must turn in faith to this Saviour, repenting of their sins. Yet that too the Old Testament Scriptures declared: that Jew and Gentile alike were to be blessed through Christ.

We may note a few details in this wonderful chapter:

Paul first insists on his unquestionable orthodoxy; he shows that Christian truth is not contrary to Jewish teaching, but that it utterly supersedes it. The Old Testament ever pointed onward to the Coming of Christ and of salvation through Him, promised of God unto the fathers. Paul says that the "twelve tribes" even then were serving God night and day. This does away with the theory of the "lost" ten tribes; they evidently were not lost when Paul spoke before Agrippa.

Paul says: "I verily thought with myself, that I ought to do many things contrary to the name of Jesus of Nazareth" (verse 9). This reminds us of the rich man of Luke 12 who also thought "within himself." It is sad indeed when one's thoughts do not leave home. God's thoughts are higher than our thoughts, as the heavens are higher than the earth.

In verse 14 we read that Jesus spoke to Paul in the Hebrew tongue. This is not mentioned elsewhere, and probably was said here to remind these Gentile hearers that, after all, the despised Jews were God's people and that He spoke their language.

As Paul speaks from the fullness of his heart of how God's gospel was committed to him to preach to both Jews and Gentiles, Festus says: "Paul, thou art beside thyself; much learning doth make thee mad." But Paul declares earnestly that he is not mad, but speaks forth the words of truth and soberness. Elsewhere he says that if he was beside himself, it was when in the presence of God alone, where he could freely let loose the pent-up passion of his soul; but before men he was sober, that the Word of God might grip them, and they not be led astray by mere emotion (see 2 Corinthians 5:13).

Paul appeals to King Agrippa as to the truth he is declaring, saying that the king knew of these things, for they were "not done in a corner" (verse 26). Praise God, Christian truth is not something palmed off on a credulous audience, but its basic facts were seen by many eyes. Christ lived His perfect life before men, and even His bitterest enemies had to admit that they could not find any sin in Him. His death was not a secret one; He was lifted up on a cross at a time when perhaps a million or more Jews were in Jerusalem at the annual Passover feast, and where thousands beheld the awe-inspiring spectacle of the sinless Saviour on a criminal's cross. He was seen after His resurrection by hundreds, who bore vigorous witness to that tremendous fact. Yes, these things were not done in a corner; there is overwhelming evidence for Christ's death and resurrection, upon which the salvation of the sinner rests.

Paul is sure that King Agrippa believed the prophets, but that does not mean that Agrippa believed on Christ. "Almost thou persuadest me to be a Christian." Almost persuaded, but lost. Agrippa may have had a sneer in his voice when he uttered those words. But Paul glories in being a Christian. This poor shackled prisoner of the Lord declares himself to be more blessed than anyone there, and fain would have them all to be such as he is, except the bonds. Agrippa did not know, nor would he have believed, that that day there stood before him one who was much more a king than he was; one who would some day reign over the whole universe, by the side of the Lord he served unto death. Paul might be a prisoner of Rome, but he was set free by the great Redeemer of souls. So are we, praise God! May we not be afraid or be slow in glorying in the cross of our Lord Jesus Christ!

27

Paul's Journey to Rome

ACTS 27

It HARDLY seems logical that this trip, with its consequent shipwreck, should be unfolded in such detail in a book like the Bible, where space is at such a premium, if it were merely to give us a historical account. But if it is given to illustrate deeper truths, then all the details assume absorbing interest. Though we cannot by any means interpret them as we would like, these details lead us to see here—in this journey from the capital city Jerusalem to the capital of Italy, Rome—a graphic pictorial record of the descent of the Church of God from Jerusalem (where it had its inception) to Rome, where eventually the Church will find its sad end, as described in the book of Revelation. We see in this trip the professing Church fall from its pristine perfection at its birth to its moral and spiritual wreck in Rome, the mother of harlots and abominations of the earth.

However obscure still the various stages, as set forth in this chapter, may be to us, the general setting is clear. Begun so propitiously, when the Holy Spirit filled the house and each individual believer at Pentecost, the Church's history ends with shipwreck; thus is Paul (and the truth he was commissioned to give us) a prisoner along the road as well as at the close.

The same sad story is seen in the seven churches from

Ephesus to the nauseating climax in Laodicea. After the happy beginning in Ephesus and the days of persecution in Smyrna, Rome appears on the scene with its Judaizing rather than Christianizing influence, coupled with the spirit of legality and its accompanying bitter animosity against the pure gospel of grace. Praise God, there have been revivals of truth during the days of the Reformation, when the simple way of salvation was once more preached; and later on the revival of the true position of the Church as the Body of Christ and the unity of all believers, with the presidency of the Holy Spirit recognized. But, in spite of all that, the journey continues steadfastly toward Rome, though slowed down by God's infinite mercy. That surely is the bird's-eye view of Acts 27, easily discernible.

Taking a broad look at this voyage, we see little fair weather, but much contrary wind and violent storms—surely typical of the Church's history. The ship pictures professing Christendom while, I judge, those aboard are meant to typify true believers. Paul and his friends comprise the smallest number of those aboard and they are prisoners; for the full truth of God is held only by the few, comparatively speaking, even among true Christians, and in general it does not find full liberty for expression.

Paul warns of damaging storms to come (verses 9-11), as he does in his Epistles so often in a spiritual sense. He speaks of perilous times to come in the last days; that after his departure grievous wolves would come in, not sparing the flock. The contrary winds then may well speak of every wind of doctrine, which toss

men to and fro by the sleight of men and cunning crafti-
ness, whereby they lie in wait to deceive (Ephesians
4:14).

But the centurion "believed the master and the owner
of the ship, more than those things which were spoken
by Paul" (verse 11). How this has found its parallel
throughout the Church's history! Men are believed who
are supposed to know, as the recognized leaders of the
great religious systems; while the truths of Scripture,
spoken by the true ministers of Christ, are ignored and
go unheeded. Well might Paul say later: "Sirs, ye should
have hearkened unto me, and not . . . have gained this
harm and loss" (verse 21).

What great loss in the spiritual life and power in the
Church would have been avoided if only the ministry
of the Apostle Paul had been heeded, as given in his
wonderful Epistles! Think of the truth presented in
the Epistle to the Galatians alone. How much the professing church has lost by failing to believe and practise
the liberty of worship and ministry which belongs to
every saint and not to a special class.

A violent storm at last burst upon them, called Euro-
clydon, but by most authorities said to be properly
named "Euroquilo," which means "northeaster." It is
easy enough to identify its spiritual meaning, for the
"east" in Scripture ever stands in its evil sense for idolatry (sun worship often being rebuked), while the
"north" has in it the idea of spiritual darkness (away
from the light), thus standing spiritually for infidelity.
Idolatry is seen prominently in Rome; infidelity in corrupt Protestantism. These buffet the Church, as so mani-

festly evident in the Church's history. Rome is noted for its idolatrous worship; Protestantism so fearfully afflicted by "modernism."

They undergirded the ship (verse 17), trying by every possible "outside" means to hold the vessel together, to keep it from falling apart. By church councils, by federal councils, lately even by the invitation of the Pope to unite again with the "true" church, men are seeking to hold the whole thing from disintegrating. Every outside means, but not the inside provision of repentance and faith in God and obedience to His Word. In the midst of all this Paul and his friends are kept in peace with God and know sweet fellowship with Him, as today is true of real believers in the midst of a corrupt, worldly religious system.

Sun nor stars appeared for many days—no light from Heaven (verse 20), and all hope of salvation is gone. Religion holds out no hope for salvation; but there is hope, and it comes from the lips of the Lord's prisoner —Paul. God's true Church, of which Paul is the representative here, has a message of cheer and hope for the world (verse 22): all that sail with Paul are given to him by his Lord (verse 24). While here of course it speaks of salvation from physical death, I believe it typifies how all those who listen to Paul—to the ministry of God's Word—shall be saved eternally.

Paul urges those on board to eat, as in their distress and anxiety they had fasted for two solid weeks. He says "ye" have fasted; apparently he himself had not. The true believer feeds on God's Word even in times of trouble and terror, perhaps more so than at any other time. But the mere religionist is starving in the midst of plenty. Paul again assures them they are secure and that not a hair shall fall from their heads. How we love the truth of the eternal security of the believer, the assurance that God's Word ever has for the ear of faith!

They cast the wheat into the sea (verse 38). The "wheat," of course, in Scripture is always a type of the Word as the "bread of life." I do not think this casting out here should be interpreted in an evil sense. I would suggest it means that they were casting the bread upon the waters now as we are told in Ecclesiastes 11:1 to do. Even though the Church itself is failing, yet through true believers the gospel is being broadcast world-wide upon the sea of nations.

All reach the shore; some swim, others cling to various pieces of the wreckage. The one Church has broken into a thousand fragments, yet all who sail with Paul, as it were, shall safely reach the shore. This is a general view illustrating the spiritual end of the Church. Perhaps some day all the details of this striking chapter will light up with beauty when our Lord Himself shall unfold them to us.

It may be said by some that the above applications are "farfetched," and I admit this. But personally I like this "farfetchedness." The virtuous woman of Proverbs 31 brought her food from afar, and if my fetching from afar will mean food to even one of God's dear saints, I shall be thankful.

The journey had two main parts: the first, the voyage and the shipwreck ending at Melita; the second, Paul's further and final journey to Rome. The first part of this trip again has two parts: first, in the ship of Adramyttium to Myra; secondly in the ship of Alexandria to Melita. Paul was a prisoner throughout; and in reality the full Christian truth of the Church as the Body of Christ and the Bride of Christ has never been fully understood by the Church as a whole.

They are bound for Italy, but not by a straight course. They started off along the coast of Asia—meaning "mire," a mixture on which one can find no sure footing, suggesting spiritual confusion and uncertainty. How the professing Church has been marked by confusion twice confounded! Contrary winds made them seek the lee of the island of Cyprus, a word meaning "blossom," specifically of the olive and the vine, identified by the Greeks with all that was fair and lovely, speaking of the soft things which appeal to the flesh. Thus we have a picture: tired of the contrary winds of persecution and opposition, finding shelter and ease in conformity with the world, as described in the address to Pergamos in Revelation 2.

Aristarchus is on board, but only as a passenger, and we hear no more of him for the rest of the journey. His name means "the best leader," but he does not do any leading; so he typifies the Holy Spirit, who is the true Leader of spiritual life, but who is largely denied that place in the Church. Like Aristarchus He is along only as a passenger and is not in charge. The Church uses the name of the Holy Spirit, but politely ignores Him and gives Him practically no authority in its service or worship.

At Myra they change to a ship of Alexandria and

thence point the prow of the ship toward Rome. Alexandria means "help given to or by man"; this well tells the story that the so-called Church of God now openly sets aside, as it were, the guidance of the Spirit through the Word, and looks to and listens to human authority for truth and the interpretation thereof. The ship is now definitely headed for Rome, where God's truth is set aside and man's thoughts and methods are substituted for it. The vessel came from Egypt, which in Scripture stands for the world and its religion and its dominance over God's people.

The wind is contrary. In mercy God slows down this inevitable descent to Rome. Then again the "south wind blew softly," and they supposed that this was what they needed; but it was soon succeeded by the violent storm that became their undoing (verses 13-14). Spiritually speaking, south winds are even more to be feared than northeasters. Times of ease and popularity were later followed by the pitiless storms of persecution, when untold numbers of saints were done to death because of their faith in Christ and defiance of Rome's heresies.

What a checkered history the Church of God has had! While on the whole it has degenerated into a professing body with very little real spiritual life, yet during the centuries millions have been saved by God's grace and have reached Heaven's shore, as these reached earth's shore. Amid the storm, the fear, the darkness, and the famine many, like Paul and his company aboard ship, believed God, rested in His love, and thus were able to bring words of cheer and preach a message of hope to the others. To Him be all the praise!

28

Paul at Melita

ACTS 28:1-10

WHAT A GLAD and yet sad contrast these verses reveal between the attitude of Paul's own nation and that of these Gentile heathen. The Jewish priests and the Roman governors present a sorrowful picture against the bright display of kindness and consideration shown by these "barbarians" of Melita. Times may have changed since then, but not the heart of man. Till this very day the religious element, as represented by the Jews throughout the book of Acts; or the political, intellectual element, as represented by the Romans; either hate or ignore the gospel appeal. Meanwhile so-called heathen, as these men of Malta, are being blessed; they receive the messengers of the Lord with respect and honor them for their work. The heathen still have an ear today, while this so-called civilized world (with exceptions, of course) closes its heart to God's matchless grace.

The barbarous people showed Paul and his company no little kindness. The chief, named Publius, received them courteously and provided room and board. The Lord rewarded them for their kindness by healing Publius' father and many others. As a result Paul and the others were highly honored in return. What a happy change this must have been to God's aged and weary servant, after having been so abused and shamed by his own nation! The months spent here were a little oasis in the desert to this dear saint. How good God is!

On to Rome

ACTS 28:11-31

FIRST PAUL was met and welcomed by the believers; next turned over to the Roman authorities; and last, he came in contact with the Jews and presented his case to them. These three receptions are again quite typical of the whole book of Acts, as well as pictorial of the last 1900 years. Paul, representative of the truth of the Church and its place and ministry on earth during this day of grace, is welcomed by the true Church; again rejected by the Jews; and imprisoned by the Gentiles. Here are the three classes as God sees them in this world: the Jew, the Gentile, and the Church of God (1 Corinthians 10:32). The Jew rejects the Christ; the Church welcomes and adores Him; Rome limits Him, keeps Him in prison as it were, and eventually gets rid of Him altogether, as will the false church in the coming day of apostasy.

Once more Paul presents the claims of Christ to his own people, the Jews, as he did so consistently and constantly, as seen throughout his ministry recorded in the book of Acts; but once more with the same result. Except for a few, his message as a whole is unwanted. Paul applies to them the very same passage describing Israel's unbelief and hardness of heart (verses 25-27) as did his Lord Himself (in Matthew 13:14-16). Israel's attitude had not changed one iota from Jesus' day till now. And once more, as throughout Acts, Paul declares that the salvation of God is sent unto the Gentiles and that they will hear it (verse 28).

The book of Acts closes abruptly. All through we read of the continuous rejection of the Saviour by the Jewish nation. It closes on the same note, except for the final sentence, which assures us that Paul for two whole years continued there, telling forth the double message which is still being preached today: the kingdom of God, and those things which concern the Lord Jesus Christ; preaching the one, and teaching the other. The "things concerning the Lord Jesus Christ" of course particularly refer to the great truths of Christianity and its full glory in the Church. So Paul preached the kingdom of God—for the gospel of God's grace received leads to new birth, and new birth introduces the soul into the kingdom of God (see John 3:3,5). Then, once they were born again, he taught the converts all the great truths concerning the Lord Jesus.

The chapter tells us nothing of Paul's future. Was he released for a while? Philippians 1:25-26 indicates that he was. Where did he go after his release and how long was it ere he was rearrested? How did he die and where? He does tell us (2 Timothy 4:6) that he would die a martyr's death, but the Scriptures give us no details. There are reasons for this silence, one of which is evident: the book of Acts is not a history of Paul, but of the Spirit's work on earth. It is written to tell us of the birth of the Church, of its early struggles, its missionary outreach, its world-wide spread. Acts gives us the transition historically from Judaism into full-blown Christianity.

May the Lord bless this brief study of Acts to our hearts, and for the enlightening of our minds, for His blessed Name's sake!

PART TWO

29

Infallible Proofs

"THE FORMER TREATISE have I made, O Theophilus, of all that Jesus began both to do and teach, until the day in which He was taken up, after that He through the Holy Ghost had given commandments unto the apostles whom He had chosen:

"To whom also He showed Himself alive after His passion by many infallible proofs, being seen of them forty days, and speaking of the things pertaining to the kingdom of God: And, being assembled together with them, commanded them that they should not depart from Jerusalem, but wait for the promise of the Father, which, saith He, ye have heard of Me.

"For John truly baptized with water; but ye shall be baptized with the Holy Ghost not many days hence. When they therefore were come together, they asked of Him, saying, Lord, wilt Thou at this time restore again the kingdom to Israel? And He said unto them, It is not for you to know the times or the seasons, which the Father hath put in His own power.

"But ye shall receive power, after that the Holy Ghost is come upon you: and ye shall be witnesses unto Me both in Jerusalem, and in all Judea, and in Samaria, and unto the uttermost part of the earth"—Acts 1:1-8

In his Gospel Luke records certain of the occasions upon which the Lord appeared to His disciples after His resurrection; in our text we have the additional information that this postgraduate course of instruction, which our Lord gave to His own, continued for a space of forty days. Ten days later, on the day of Pentecost, which means "fiftieth"—that is, fifty days after the Lord's resurrection—the Spirit came down from Heaven, in accordance with the promise the Lord had made in the Gospels, and formed the believers into the One Body—the Church, as well as indwelt every individual believer to empower them for Christian life and service.

Jesus had laid the foundation for all blessing in His precious death on the cross (a work which He alone could accomplish), but He had also begun (Acts 1:1) a work which His disciples were to carry on, after He Himself had been "taken up" (verse 2). That work is still unfinished—the work of building His Church through the salvation of souls—a work in which, praise His Name, He enlists the service of every believer. It is our great privilege to have a part in the great work of leading souls to Christ and thus of seeing them added to the Church, that they may be built as living stones into a spiritual house, which is the Church of the living God.

The Lord Jesus showed Himself alive to His own for forty days, instructing them and preparing them for His service ere He Himself went home to glory. Our blessed Lord showed He was truly God's Man—the champion of the needy human race—by defeating Satan so decisively during the forty days of temptation in the wilderness prior to His public life on earth; He proved He had done so by walking with His own forty days after His triumphant resurrection. What a wonderful postgraduate course those six weeks must have been to His faithful followers!

In order to fit His saints for such a responsible task, divine provision had to be made; provision of which the verses of our present text speak. Notice that before Jesus was taken up to Heaven He furnished His own with three mighty helps in their warfare against Satan; these are brought to our attention by the threefold use of the word "after":

"After He through the Holy Ghost had given commandments"—verse 2.

"After His passion He showed Himself alive by many infallible proofs"—verse 3.

"After the Holy Ghost is come upon you"—verse 8.

Here is a threefold provision that will enable any believer to be a faithful and courageous servant of Christ: 1, precepts; 2, passion; 3, power. The Word of God furnishes the divine guidance and instruction for every spiritual need and every circumstance; the love of God furnishes the needed passion and devotion; and the Holy Spirit fully supplies the divine power to those who in themselves are but weak creatures, but who can do all things by the power of the indwelling Holy Spirit. These three furnish the complete man unto all good works: the Word enlightens the spirit; the passion stirs the soul; and the Holy Spirit activates the movements of the body. Here truly is perfect enablement.

Our blessed Lord Himself exemplified all this so wonderfully in His own life and death. The Word of God was ever His guide and charter; He did all by the power of the Spirit (Acts 10:38); and how could we ever speak adequately of the holy passion that led Him all the way to Calvary? Love was the motive force with Him—love to God and love for man.

He *showed Himself* alive. All through the four Gospels we are bidden to behold how life should be lived. Example is so much more potent than precept, and so our gracious God has seen fit to give us a fourfold record of the life of Christ that we might see as well as hear eternal life. I feel that Christians should study the four Gospels more than they do, for in them we *see* the truths which we *hear* in the Epistles. Example, as we all know, is so much more effective than precept. For the forty days after His resurrection our Lord once more gave His disciples a course in true holy living and effective service. During those days the Lord had a new body, a glorified body—suited to Heaven—by which He could enter through locked doors, and appear or vanish at will (Luke 24:31). Shall we say that He walked in a new way—in newness of life? Even so our walk in a spiritual way is to be different as now we walk among men as those who have been raised from the dead and are possessors of a new life.

Notice the remarkable expression in the third verse of our text—He showed Himself *alive*. That word caught my attention years ago. How else could He show *Himself* except alive? That word *alive* savors of tautology if we see here only a reference to Christ

Himself. For, if He were dead He could not show Himself; in that case others would have to show Him. Applying this to Christ alone, the word *alive* has no place in the sentence; all it would need to say is that He showed Himself. But I believe there is precious suggestive truth in the use here of this word *alive*. The Lord Jesus in this verse, as in His entire life, is set forth as an example for us to follow His steps. As He showed Himself alive in a physical way, so we are to show ourselves alive spiritually.

Here is where this word *alive* becomes alive with meaning; we Christians, spiritually speaking, *can* show ourselves dead and alive, either way, since the Scripture tells us that we are both dead and alive (Romans 6:11). Once we were dead in sins; now we are to be dead to sin and alive unto God. We are dead to sins (1 Peter 2:24) judicially in the sight of God; and we are to make this practically true in our daily lives by living a life of dependence upon divine power and grace. But there is always the danger and possibility of our drifting away from the Lord; when we do, we show forth the old life and nature; thus we would show ourselves dead instead of alive. I believe that is why the word *alive* is included in our text. When a believer lives a carnal life he shows himself dead instead of showing himself alive. Romans 8:6 says to be carnally minded is *death*. It is sadly possible for a believer to show himself spiritually dead instead of alive.

One of the surest ways to *seem* dead (for a real Christian of course is never actually dead spiritually) is to go to sleep. Hence the New Testament has a number of warnings against believers going to sleep in that way, as in 1 Thessalonians 5:6; Luke 22:46; Ephesians 5:14, etc. When a Christian is asleep on the job he appears to be dead, for at a little distance it is impossible to tell dead and sleeping persons apart. A sleeping Christian and a dead sinner look sadly alike—often it is impossible to tell which is which.

And so the call comes from God: "Awake thou that sleepest, and arise from among the dead, and Christ shall give thee light" (Ephesians 5:14). This is God's rousing call to the sleeping Christian: "Show thyself alive." If a number of people—of both dead and sleeping ones—were lying down, you could not tell them apart; but the moment you saw one stand up, you would know he anyway was not dead—he would be showing himself alive. An upstanding Christian is thus a true testimony for Christ.

An "alive" Christian is a testimony for Christ and will be used of Him to the blessing of souls. After Lazarus had been raised from the dead by our Lord, it is not recorded that he ever spoke again; Scripture never says that he spoke of his experience during the time his soul was absent from his body, yet we read that "because of him many went away and believed on Jesus" (John 12:11, 17-19). The very fact that he was alive proved the power of Christ; and it is so in your case and mine. Christians who live Christ magnify Christ.

The story is told of two men who walked into a taxidermist's shop. While waiting to be waited on, one began to criticize the various displays.

"Look at this parrot, for instance. You never see a parrot holding his head in that odd way, nor grasp a perch in this peculiar manner." Just then the parrot spoke up and said, "Oh, is that so?" It happened to be a live parrot; by the very fact that he was alive, he instantly killed all the criticism, and crushed the criticizer. So it will be if we show ourselves alive.

The Lord showed Himself alive, the Scripture says, by many infallible proofs, and we, even in our little capacity, can do the same in our spiritual life. Note some of the ways our Lord showed Himself—some of the unmistakable proofs of spiritual aliveness:

1. He was seen. So should we be seen; in fact, we are seen every day; as people see us, they should see likeness to our blessed Lord in all our ways.

2. He spoke to them of the things pertaining to the kingdom of God. Speaking is one of the strongest proofs of spiritual life. It is amazing what a part speech plays in everyday living; also in spiritual testimony. Speaking is constantly presented in Scripture as evidence of the fullness of the Spirit (Acts 2:4; 4:8; 4:31; etc., etc.). In these and in many verses throughout the Bible we read that when believers were filled with the Spirit they spoke. Out of the abundance of the heart the mouth speaks.

3. Jesus walked and talked with the two on the way to Emmaus, and was known of them in the breaking of bread. We too can show ourselves alive by walking in harmony and fellowship with believers and by often speaking one to another.

4. He ate and drank with the disciples after He rose

from the dead (Acts 10:41). So we show ourselves alive by remembering the Lord in the breaking of the bread; in eating and drinking with fellow saints, with Jesus in our midst.

5. He blessed them in their work and ministered to their need, as He stood on the shore of the lake of Galilee (John 21). So we can encourage and cheer others, and meet their physical needs when they are cold and hungry.

6. He restored erring Simon Peter, when He met him alone that first day after He had risen, as intimated in Luke 24:34. What a privilege it is to show ourselves spiritually alive by seeking to restore those who have fallen by the wayside; especially to do this in meekness and gentleness, considering ourselves, lest we also be tempted (Galatians 6:1).

7. He showed Himself alive by drying Mary's tears and comforting her, then sending her on a mission to tell others that she had seen the Lord. We, if spiritually alive, may do the same. There are many tears that need drying; many persons who, when comforted, can carry a message of comfort and joy to others, as did Mary.

Yes, in these and no doubt in many other ways, Jesus showed Himself alive after His death and resurrection, setting us an example to follow in His steps. And then He went to glory (when His work here was done), as we too shall be caught up someday—to be forever with Him where He is! Till then, may we show ourselves "alive"!

30

The Upper Room

"And when He had spoken these things, while they beheld, He was taken up; and a cloud received Him out of their sight. And while they looked stedfastly toward heaven as He went up, behold, two men stood by them in white apparel; which also said, Ye men of Galilee, why stand ye gazing up into heaven? this same Jesus, which is taken up from you into heaven, shall so come in like manner as ye have seen Him go into heaven.

"Then returned they unto Jerusalem from the mount called Olivet, which is from Jerusalem a sabbath day's journey.

"And when they were come in, they went up into an upper room, where abode both Peter, and James, and John, and Andrew, Philip, and Thomas, Bartholomew, and Matthew, James the son of Alphaeus, and Simon Zelotes, and Judas the brother of James.

"These all continued with one accord in prayer and supplication, with the women, and Mary the mother of Jesus, and with His brethren"—Acts 1:9-14

When the disciples returned to Jerusalem from the Mount of Olives, where the Lord had just left them— to return to His Father in Heaven—blessing them with outstretched hands as He ascended (Luke 24:51), they went up into an upper room. On the night of His betrayal they had celebrated the Passover, and the Lord Jesus had instituted the Lord's Supper—which would be enjoyed by His saints throughout the centuries—also in an upper room, furnished (Mark 14:15). From this upper room—by the way of Gethsemane, Golgotha, and Olivet—the Lord's own loved ones had now assembled once more in an *upper room*. In this upper room they abode for ten days, waiting for the descent of the Holy Spirit, as the Lord Jesus had commanded them to do, for He had said to them: "Behold, I send the promise of My Father upon you: but tarry ye in the city of Jerusalem, until ye be endued with power from on high" (Luke 24:49).

The "upper room" thus seems to have a significant meaning in Christian life. We find it again in Acts 20:7-8 when the disciples came together to break bread. These came from the Mount of Olives where they were above the city of Jerusalem on its outside, into the upper room where they were above the city on the inside. That truly is the proper position for the believer in Jesus at any time: in the world, but not of it; in it, but, as they were, above it. "Up" and "above" are pertinent things in a believer's spiritual experience. Christianity is heavenly; it lifts the believer above this world, on a higher moral and spiritual level, in communion with God and with His saints. Then, in the midst of that religious city that had just crucified its Messiah; today, in the world that has little more real use for Christ; the believer occupies a spiritual eminence—with doors that shut out the world and its ways, and shuts in the true saints with God.

It is interesting to note that Luke's Gospel completely passes over these ten days in the upper room—these ten days between the ascension of Christ and the descent of the Holy Spirit. In Luke 24 it reads as if the apostles and other believers went immediately from the Mount of Olives to Jerusalem, and were continually in the Temple, praising and blessing God (Luke 24:52-53). Yet Acts 1:13 shows that they did *not* go to the Temple, but went into the upper room, where they abode the whole ten days that intervened between the Lord's ascension and the day of Pentecost. It is not till after Pentecost that we read they went into the Temple, according to Acts 2:46: "And they, continuing daily with one accord in the temple. . . ." Careful comparison will show that the last verse of Luke's Gospel records the same events as Acts 2:46, just quoted. Luke omits the mention of those intervening ten days of Acts 1:13 altogether. God's Word is perfect and records or omits facts for special reasons.

I believe the ten-day period of prayer in the upper room, as given in Acts 1:13, is left out by Luke because Luke's Gospel deals with the Lord's ministry toward His saints, while Acts speaks of our ministry for Him. In connection with our ministry, prayer is such a vital necessity; hence the emphasis on the ten days of prayer in the book of Acts. So also we read in Luke that Jesus ascended from Bethany—which was the place where our Lord so often enjoyed sweet fellowship with Mary and Martha. Luke hence mentions Bethany, for his Gospel is the account of Christ as Man walking in fellowship with men. In Acts it is said that Jesus ascends from the Mount of Olives (both of course refer to the same spot, for Bethany was situated on the Mount of Olives), because the olive produced the oil which in Scripture is often a type of the fullness of the Spirit of God. Hence the Mount of Olives is mentioned in Acts, because these disciples in the upper room were waiting for the Spirit —the Spirit so necessary for successful Christian service; and service is the theme in the book of Acts.

Note also in Luke that as Jesus went up He blessed them, and as a result they worshiped Him. This, I believe, is the first time in the New Testament we read that the Lord Jesus was worshiped directly by His disciples. While Christ was on earth He directed worship to the Father, but now that He is ascended and glorified, worship properly is extended to the Son as well.

In Acts, as the disciples stand gazing up into Heaven after Jesus' farewell to them, the two men say to them: "Why stand ye gazing up into heaven?" This question is not raised in Luke, for it is proper for faith to gaze upon an ascended Lord in glory, in order to enjoy fullest fellowship with Him; and we remember that fellowship is specially Luke's theme. But service is the keynote of Acts, so here heaven-gazing must be exchanged for a look on the fields; fields which are ready for the preaching of the message of God's redeeming love.

The fact that Luke omits the ten days entirely, and goes right on from the Lord's ascension to the Spirit's descent and the stirring events of Pentecost, explains the otherwise inexplicable behavior of the disciples as given in Luke 24:52 where it is said that from Bethany they returned to Jerusalem with "great joy." They had been so sad when Christ had died (Luke 24:17); how then could they be so full of joy now when they had just said good-by to their dearest Friend, never again to see Him on earth?

The answer to this problem is very simple when again we remind ourselves that they did not return to Jerusalem and go into the Temple till *after* Pentecost (Acts 2:46). It happened after Pentecost, after the Holy Ghost had come upon them. By that time, by the Spirit, their eyes had been opened to the truths that prior to the coming of the Spirit they did not seem able to comprehend, as the Lord Himself had told them in John 16:12-13: "I have yet many things to say unto you, but ye cannot bear them now. Howbeit when He, the Spirit of truth, is come, He will guide you into all truth. . . ." That Spirit had now come upon them; their eyes were opened to the real worth and glory of Him with whom they had walked. Now they understood the infinite value of His precious death, glorious resurrection, and triumphant ascension. Now they understood the wonder of a glorified Christ in Heaven, ever to intercede for them, with the power and enlightenment of the indwelling Spirit on earth. No wonder they were filled with joy. So we, though we do not see Jesus either, with the eyes of our heads, yet we do see Him by faith at God's right hand; and so we too know something of joy unspeakable and full of glory.

How lovely to see that in Mark's Gospel, after they returned from the Lord's ascension, they *preached;* for

Mark is the Gospel of ministry (Mark 16:15). In Luke, after His ascension, they *praised;* for Luke is the Gospel of fellowship. In Acts, after they returned, they *prayed;* which is so needed for a life to be lived for Him. They worked in the world; they praised in His presence; they prayed in the assembly, with the fellowship of other saints.

They prayed for ten days in the upper room, waiting for the promised Spirit. The eleven apostles were there, a number of those sisters who were so true to Christ and ministered to Him while He was on earth. (I wonder if the sisters outnumbered the brethren among these one hundred and twenty, as they so frequently do to-day?) There was Jesus' mother, mentioned specially, and His "brethren." Since other men were mentioned before, it seems logical to conclude that these "brethren" were the Lord's brothers after the flesh. Apparently, during the Lord's life, the other sons of Mary did not believe in Christ (John 7:5); one loves to think that His death, miraculous resurrection, and no less miraculous ascension at last had opened their eyes to recognize Him as *their* Saviour and Lord.

Altogether there were one hundred and twenty present at this ten-day prayer meeting (Acts 1:15). Where were the rest? We read in 1 Corinthians 15 that at least five hundred had been saved during Christ's preaching of the gospel. One would like to believe that the room was not large enough to accommodate all of these, and that the other three hundred and eighty were unable to get in. But we know, alas, that in our own day, one hundred and twenty out of a possible five hundred is a sad but true ratio for our prayer meetings.

We might say that only the men prayed, for the pronoun "these," who continued in prayer, is in the masculine form. Even then it seems 1 Timothy 2: 8,12 was practised.

They weren't much—this little group in an upper room, setting themselves apart from the properly recognized religion of that day—were they? There were no "big shots" there; no Herod, no Pilate, no chief priest. Not many or perhaps not any mighty or noble; just the ordinary garden variety of humans: humble fishermen, despised publicans. None had been to college; they were not educated or ordained. But they were in high favor with Heaven. They were God's elite. Christ's interests were paramount here. Ask Peter or John what they think of Him! Anything or anyone against the Lord Jesus Christ would have been highly resented and rejected in that society. They prayed; they felt their need of prayer. They waited upon God and ere long the power fell.

They were in that upper room "with one accord." Five times that expression "with one accord" is found in connection with the coming of the Spirit and the believer's attitude to Christ. One cannot help but think that if one hundred and twenty believers could again pray for ten days with one accord, once more the mighty power of God would be seen and heard.

Brethren, let us pray!

31

The Field of Blood

"And in those days Peter stood up in the midst of the disciples, and said, (the number of names together were about an hundred and twenty,) Men and brethren, this scripture must needs have been fulfilled, which the Holy Ghost by the mouth of David spake before concerning Judas, which was guide to them that took Jesus. For he was numbered with us, and had obtained part of this ministry.

"Now this man purchased a field with the reward of iniquity; and falling headlong, he burst asunder in the midst, and all his bowels gushed out. And it was known unto all the dwellers at Jerusalem; insomuch as that field is called in their proper tongue, Aceldama, that is to say, The field of blood.

"For it is written in the book of Psalms, Let his habitation be desolate, and let no man dwell therein: and his bishopric let another take.

"Wherefore of these men which have companied with us all the time that the Lord Jesus went in and out among us, beginning from the baptism of John, unto that same day that He was taken up from us, must one be ordained to be a witness with us of His resurrection. And they appointed two, Joseph called Barsabas, who was surnamed Justus, and Matthias. And they prayed, and said,

Thou, Lord, which knowest the hearts of all men, shew whether of these two Thou hast chosen, that he may take part of this ministry and apostleship, from which Judas by transgression fell, that he might go to his own place.

"And they gave forth their lots; and the lot fell upon Matthias; and he was numbered with the eleven apostles" —Acts 1:15-26

There are, we might say, four "fields of blood" mentioned in the Scriptures, all of them, I think, with direct reference to the blood of our Lord Jesus Christ. In each case the *field* refers to the world (see Matthew 13: 38), of which it is a type, for the world is stained with the blood of the precious Son of God.

There is Cain's field of blood (read Genesis 4:8-15). He wantonly slew his brother Abel. It is very clear in the Bible that Abel is a picture of Christ (Hebrews 12: 24), whose innocent blood was shed by the hand of him who stands for man in his pride and self-will and religious self-righteousness. But Cain also stands more directly for the nation of Israel, which, as happened to Cain, consequent to the murder of their Abel—Christ—became fugitive and vagabond in the earth. The field became saturated with the blood of Abel, as this world has become with the precious blood of Christ. As the Lord told Cain that "the voice of thy brother's blood crieth unto Me from the ground," so the blood of the Lord Jesus, shed at Calvary, and soaking into the earth at the foot of the cross, calls to God for vengeance on those who trample it under foot. But, praise God, it also calls to God for the blessing of all who shelter beneath its cleansing power.

There is the field of blood mentioned in Deuteronomy 21:1-9. When a man was found slain in the land of Israel, lying in the field, the elders and the judges of the nation were to take an heifer on which no yoke had ever come, shed its blood, and then wash their hands over the heifer and say, "Our hands have not shed this blood, neither have our eyes seen it. Be merciful, O Lord, unto Thy people Israel, whom Thou hast redeemed, and lay not innocent blood unto Thy people of Israel's charge." On such occasions they might be able to pray thus, but not so could those of Israel who crucified the Son of God. That slain person found in the field speaks of Him who was ruthlessly murdered by His own people Israel; that heifer upon which no yoke had come typifies Him also. The murdered man speaks of the Christ whom Israel rejected; the heifer upon which no yoke had come speaks of the same Person as God; and by faith we see Him—the holy, spotless Son of God, who in matchless love gave Himself willingly a sacrifice for sin—theirs and ours.

Israel cannot wash her hands in water (nor could Pilate, as he professed to do) and say: "Our hands have not shed this blood, neither have our eyes seen it." It *was* their hands that shed His blood, as Stephen said in Acts 7:52: "Of whom ye have now been the betrayers and murderers." They could not say. "Our eyes have not seen it," for they were there, standing around His cross in mockery and saying: "If Thou be the Christ, the chosen of God, come down from the cross and we will believe." They could not say that they were innocent of His death. The field is stained with blood, in the shedding of which they were dreadfully guilty; blood that has come upon them and on their children, as they so recklessly prayed. There was innocent blood, but it was not theirs; it was His. Not as long as Israel pleads innocent, but only when she pleads guilty, shall that fearful stain be removed and forgiveness come.

Pilate, the representative of the Gentiles, also claimed innocence in the crime of the shedding of the blood of Christ. Like Israel, he too washed his hands in innocence, while giving the Innocent One into the vile hands of wicked men, to shame and dishonor and fearful suffering. When Pilate was claiming innocence he was deliberately closing his eyes to his inexcusable crime. But so it had to be, for both Israel and the Gentiles banded together against the Lord and against His Christ (Acts 4:27).

There is the field of blood our blessed Lord purchased Himself when He laid down His life in sacrifice. Matthew 13:38 tells us that the field is the world and verse 44 of that chapter tells us that He laid aside everything —for He who was rich, for our sakes become poor—to buy that field. He bought this world with the price of His precious blood; the world and all that is therein, is His by right of purchase.

We have the field of blood once more brought before us in the history of Judas in our present text (Acts 1:19). Three times the purchase of this field is mentioned. First in Zechariah 11:12-13. While the direct buying of the field is not given there, the quotation from that chapter, as found in Matthew 27:9-10, shows the money was used to buy the potter's field and it was henceforth called the "field of blood." Next we learn from Matthew 27: 5-8 that the priests used the money, which Judas returned, for the purchase of this field. Then in Acts 1:18 we find that the purchase of this field is attributed to Judas. The Lord Himself is seen as the buyer in Zechariah 11, for it was He who overruled man's vile wickedness for the carrying out of His own wise purposes of grace. In Matthew 27 the purchase is attributed to the priests who did the actual buying. Finally it is charged to Judas who contributed the cash.

What a price Israel paid for the crucifixion of the Son of God: it secured for them dispersion throughout the whole world, and the unceasing spilling of their blood throughout the centuries. The Lord shall come someday to "make inquisition for blood" (Psalm 9:12). Then shall the curse be lifted and the blood, instead of being a curse to Israel, shall become, as she turns in repentance to Christ, the ground for her eternal blessing, as it is now for everyone who believes in Jesus.

Notice the following contrasts:

1. Christ and Judas both bought a field.—Acts 1:18; Matthew 13:44

Judas bought it with the reward of his own iniquity. —Acts 1:18

Our Lord bought it with the wages of sin (not His, but our sins).

2. Judas took his life—driven to it by his own guilt. Jesus gave His life—for the sins of others.

3. Judas' purchase was used to buy a field to bury "strangers" in. Israel was driven out of her land, and for nineteen centuries strangers lived and died in it, while Israel died outside of it.

Christ bought it (the world) not for a cemetery, but someday to make it a national home for Israel; not to bury dead strangers in, but for the enjoyment of living saints.

4. Its purchase is attributed to the Lord.—Zechariah 11:13

To the priests.—Matthew 27:7

To Judas.—Acts 1:18

5. Matthew 27:7-8 shows it was called the field of blood, with reference to the innocent blood of Christ.

Acts 1:19 shows it was called the field of blood because of the guilty blood of Judas. Both are true. Where sin abounded, grace did much more abound.

6. Judas committed suicide, hanging himself.

Our Lord was ignominiously hanged on a tree, bearing our curse; but thus, praise God, He gave His life to give us life.

7. Judas' bowels gushed out after he fell to his death.

Our blessed Lord poured forth His bowels of infinite compassion as He hung upon the cross. He poured out His soul unto death.—Isaiah 53:12

Zechariah 11 and Matthew 27 reveal that the money of His betrayal was used to buy the potter's field, Zechariah adding that the money was cast to the potter, apparently so that the potter might use this field in his work. And that is precisely what the Word of God teaches as to God's dealings with Israel. In Jeremiah 18 we learn that Israel is spoken of as clay and the Lord as the Potter. Israel is like a vessel that is marred, that is good for nothing and needs to be made over completely new; in other words—needs to be born again. This is exactly what the Lord purposes to do with Israel, as He says in verse 6 of that chapter: "O house of Israel, cannot I do with you as this potter? Behold, as the clay is in the potter's hand, so are ye in Mine hand, O house of Israel." God does the same thing with any individual soul. We have become marred through sin, and the great Potter makes us anew, saves us by His grace, so we may be to the display of His glory forever.

Jeremiah deals specially with Israel in that way. Judas bought the clay when he bought the field and made the world, through his fearful crime, a world of blood, specially for Israel. But there is hope. The world is a potter's field, where the Redeemer of Israel shall yet form a nation out of earthly clay, to be His earthly redeemed people. That blood, spilled by wicked Judas (his very name represents the nation of Judah—the Jews), yet so graciously offered in atoning sacrifice by our Lord, shall yet be the basis for a newborn Israel in this world. That which for centuries has been used as a graveyard for strangers, shall yet become the stage where Christ and His people Israel shall be displayed to wondering worlds. God will turn the exceeding wickedness of men into an occasion for filling Heaven and earth with His praises. The Potter shall make use of the clay to fashion millions of vessels for His glory, that all men may say: "What hath God wrought!"

32

Simon Peter's Deliverance

"Now ABOUT that time Herod the king stretched forth his hands to vex certain of the church. And he killed James the brother of John with the sword. And because he saw it pleased the Jews, he proceeded further to take Peter also. (Then were the days of unleavened bread.) And when he had apprehended him, he put him in prison, and delivered him to four quaternions of soldiers to keep him; intending after Easter to bring him forth to the people. Peter therefore was kept in prison: but prayer was made without ceasing of the church unto God for him.

"And when Herod would have brought him forth, the same night Peter was sleeping between two soldiers, bound with two chains: and the keepers before the door kept the prison. And, behold, the angel of the Lord came upon him, and a light shined in the prison: and he smote him on the side, and raised him up, saying, Arise up quickly. And his chains fell off from his hands. And the angel said unto him, Gird thyself, and bind on thy sandals. And so he did. And he saith unto him, Cast thy garment about thee, and follow me.

"And he went out, and followed him; and wist not that it was true which was done by the angel; but thought he saw a vision. When they were past the first and the second ward, they came unto the iron gate that leadeth unto the city; which opened to them of his own accord; and they went out, and passed on through one street; and forthwith the angel departed from him.

"And when Peter was come to himself, he said, Now I know of a surety, that the Lord hath sent His angel, and hath delivered me out of the hand of Herod, and from all the expectation of the people of the Jews. And when he had considered the thing, he came to the house of Mary the mother of John, whose surname was Mark; where many were gathered together praying.

"And as Peter knocked at the door of the gate, a damsel came to hearken, named Rhoda. And when she knew Peter's voice, she opened not the gate for gladness, but ran in, and told how Peter stood before the gate. And they said unto her, Thou art mad. But she constantly affirmed that it was even so. Then said they, It is his angel.

"But Peter continued knocking: and when they had opened the door, and saw him, they were astonished. But he, beckoning unto them with the hand to hold their peace, declared unto them how the Lord had brought him out of the prison. And he said, Go shew these things unto James, and to the brethren. And he departed, and went into another place."—Acts 12: 1-17

The details of Peter's deliverance from the prison and from the power of Herod may well have spiritual implications, for I believe that the Word of God always says much more than appears on the surface. I believe that this whole story has its counterpart spiritually in the deliverance of the soul from the power of sin and Satan into the liberty and blessing of redemption.

1. Peter was in prison; not for any sin of his own, of course, yet it may picture how all men are prisoners. Our souls were once in the prison house of sin, from which the Lord in His grace has set us free, for He proclaims "liberty to the captives, and the opening of the prison to them that are bound" (Isaiah 61:1); "the Lord looseth the prisoners" (Psalm 146:7).

Sometimes too the believer feels, as it were, shut up in prison, as did David in Psalm 142:7, when he prayed to the Lord to bring his soul out of prison that he might praise His Name. In either case, deliverance comes from God, as it did to Peter in this Roman jail.

2. Peter's plight seemed hopeless, from a human point of view. So is the sinner's condition apart from the mighty grace and power of God. Peter was guarded by two soldiers, one on each side. He was bound with two chains to those two men, and there were two more keepers outside of the door. The two on the inside may well speak of the two that bind the sinner within: a guilty conscience and a condemning memory (Romans 2:15); both of these bearing witness to the helpless, hopeless state of the soul. Those two on the outside, I believe, typify the mighty enemies of the soul without: the world with its attractions and delusions and Satan with his false religious deceptions. Every sinner is thus held a helpless prisoner by the cords of his sins—the lusts of the flesh and the mind within, and by the mighty

powers around and above him that bind him with chains impossible for man to break.

Then there was the locked and barred door, which is the worst of all, for it speaks of man's heart tightly closed against the appeal of God's love; a door outside of which the Saviour stands as He knocks for admittance.

Furthermore, it was the last night on earth for Peter, so it seemed. It was to be then or never. Praise God, man's need furnishes God's opportunity for blessing. The dying thief was saved at the last hour; Peter was saved the last night; and many a sinner has been saved at the last minute.

3. The angel came on the scene; the angel of the Lord. Could it have been the Lord Jesus Himself? Why not, since so often in Scripture He is designated as "the" angel of the Lord? In the hour of His death, there was none to deliver Him. No, He died alone, forsaken, that thus He might be able to deliver millions not merely from physical death, as with Peter here, but from the eternal death of everlasting doom.

The angel came and a light shined in the prison. The light of the knowledge of the glory of God in the face of Jesus Christ shines into the dark hearts of men; the light of the grace of God as it shines forth from God's holy Word. But alas, many never see it, as in the case of these soldiers. They slept right through it, though the light shone brightly all about them. The god of this world blinds the minds of them that believe not, lest the light of the gospel of the glory of Christ should shine into them.

The light came first, revealing Peter's helpless state. So the light of God's Word first of all must reveal the sinner's lost condition, as it did Peter's in that dark dungeon. And then God's Word in its bright light also shows forth God's wonderful love and saving power.

4. The angel smote Peter on the side. This verb "smite" is the same as in Acts 12:23, where it represented the stroke of judgment that destroyed wicked king Herod. It is the same word as in Matthew 26:31, where it refers to the judgment our Saviour bore for us at Calvary. Thus in the smiting of Peter we should read a hint of the judgment that by right should fall on the sinner, but which fell in wondrous grace on the Saviour who took the sinner's place. The awful judgment of sin and the wondrous love of Christ, that made Him bear that judgment for us, should awaken every sinner from the sleep of death, as it awoke Peter here.

The angel smote Peter "on the side," where the heart is located. Again how this reminds us of our blessed Lord! Wasn't His side smitten for us, that the great love of God might flow down to us? Peter was smitten on the side, as it were, to recall to him the smiting of His Lord. So the piercing of our Saviour at Calvary should stir the heart of every sinner and awaken them to open their hearts to God's great love. Yes, the gospel of the grace of God appeals to the heart of man (not to his mind specially), for with the heart man believeth unto righteousness. That is why Peter was smitten on the side by the angel. That smiting should speak of the sacrificial "death" of Christ for sinners.

This in turn is followed by:

5. He raised him up, saying, "Arise up quickly." Death is followed by resurrection. He whose side was smitten for our redemption, rose again for our justification. This death and resurrection is here in figure applied to Peter, for the smiting is succeeded by the rising up. We have died with Him; we now rise with Him to newness of life. The angel calls on Peter to respond—to get up. He might have replied that he could not, that he was fastened to those two guards with heavy manacles; but he did nothing of the kind. God's commands are God's enablements; and so Peter rose. The same thing happens in the conversion of the sinner.

6. The chains fell off. "My chains are snapped; the power of sin is broken, and I am free." How marvelous! How simple! The soldiers knew nothing about it; were entirely oblivious to it all. When the sinner obeys the gospel, all his sins are gone; the power that limited his life is broken and he is free to walk, to live, for God's glory. Do it "quickly," said the angel. Now is the accepted time; do not delay! The King's business requireth haste.

7. Gird thyself . . . bind on thy sandals . . . cast thy garment about thee . . . follow me. Till now the angel had done it all, for salvation is entirely of the Lord. But now Peter is told what his responsibility is to be. Once the soul is saved, there are responsibilities to be met. The angel tells him to do four things: four things which every saved soul is also expected to obey.

Gird thyself. We are told to gird our loins with truth

(Ephesians 6:14); to gird up the loins of our mind (1 Peter 1:13). This means that, once saved, we are henceforth to make up our minds to walk lives that honor Him; to set our minds on things above, where Christ sits at the right hand of God.

Bind on thy sandals. God gives us the capacity to carry the message of love to others. Our feet are shod with the preparation of the gospel of peace. Peter was about to go forth to resume his life, marching through this rough, wicked world, so he needed to be well shod. And as we go, we spread the story of God's love; "How beautiful are the feet of them that carry the gospel of peace"!

Put on thy garment. A familiar simile in Scripture is the garment for a Christlike life. We are urged to put on the Lord Jesus Christ as a garment that will display the loveliness of Christ (Romans 13:14); we are by His grace "all dressed up in Jesus." We are to put off the old man and to put on the new; something which is illustrated in our baptism, when we are buried with Christ: we bury the old man, and henceforth walk in newness of life.

Follow Me. That sums up the whole thing. Now we are no longer left to our own devices, to find our own way. Jesus is the Captain of our salvation; by the power of the Spirit we now live a life of devotion and Christlikeness. He is our Example—the One whose steps we are to follow.

8. The iron gate opened to them "of his own accord." The magic of the electric eye is not as new as some folks

might think; the Bible is not only up to date but far ahead of date. How many a difficulty and problem opens "of his own accord" to God's people, when they follow on obediently under the guidance of the Lord by His Spirit.

9. Now at last Peter came to himself (verse 11). He said: "Now I know!" One never comes to oneself till one has first come to Christ. The sinner is beside himself; the believer, like the prodigal of Luke 15, comes to himself when he returns to God in repentance. And God uses self, once it has been surrendered to Him. Self plays a large part in even the Christian's life. God uses *our* self to display *Him*self. We are to present our bodies to Him as a living sacrifice, holy, acceptable unto Him, which is our intelligent service. And, as we yield ourselves to Him, we learn to know His mind, for Peter could say too, "*Now* I *know.*" I, too, as a believer in Jesus can say with joy, "Now I know." I know Him whom to know is life eternal. I know His Word, while I daily keep on knowing more, and shall do so, as endless ages roll. Praise God, when one believes God, one really knows. The Bible is the Book of true knowledge.

10. Peter considered all that had happened (verse 12). Then he made his decision as to what to do next. The angel of the Lord had left him after doing for him what Peter could not do for himself; now he was to use his own judgment. God works so with us today. He does not tell us what to do in every given case or circumstance in our life, but lays down in Scripture certain divine principles; then leaves us to use our own spiritual

judgment. We must find what the will of God is for us by personal exercise of heart and mind, while seeking light from God's Word to direct us aright.

11. Peter told the whole story of his experience to the saints gathered at Mary's home (verse 17); and told them to rehearse it, in turn, to the rest of the brethren who were not there. So it is well to repeat the wondrous story of the delivering mercy of God, for the comfort and encouragement of God's dear people.

It has been remarked by many that the saints prayed for Peter, then were astonished when he knocked at the door; and this has been given as a sign of lack of faith. I do not say this is not so; however, we might note that it does not say that they prayed for Peter's deliverance, but simply that they prayed for him. I have wondered whether they may only have prayed for Peter, that he might have strength and grace to meet the ordeal he was to face the next day—the ordeal of his execution; the more so because they knew that no deliverance had come in for James, the brother of John. If this be so, it would still show lack of faith, in a way even more reprehensible, for then they did not even have any hope at all that God would intervene on Peter's behalf.

Peter slept peacefully during what for him might have been his last night on earth. It has been suggested by some, and it seems logical, that Peter slept like a child because he *knew* he would *not* die the next day. The Lord had plainly told him (in John 21:18) that he could not die a martyr's death till he was an old man; and since he was not old yet on this occasion, therefore he could not die. I wonder whether Peter remembered that promise of his Lord that particular night? All of us have the assurance from God that nothing can happen to any of His own unless He says so; "our times are in His Hand"—not in the hands of men.

These are some of the lessons we may profit by, as gleaned from this deliverance of Simon Peter. May the Lord sanctify them to us!

33

The Conversion of the Philippian Jailor

"AND WHEN her masters saw that the hope of their gains was gone, they caught Paul and Silas, and drew them into the marketplace unto the rulers, and brought them to the magistrates, saying, These men, being Jews, do exceedingly trouble our city, and teach customs, which are not lawful for us to receive, neither to observe, being Romans. And the multitude rose up together against them: and the magistrates rent off their clothes, and commanded to beat them. And when they had laid many stripes upon them, they cast them into prison, charging the jailor to keep them safely: who, having received such a charge, thrust them into the inner prison, and made their feet fast in the stocks.

"And at midnight Paul and Silas prayed, and sang praises to God: and the prisoners heard them. And suddenly there was a great earthquake, so that the foundations of the prison were shaken: and immediately all the doors were opened, and every one's bands were loosed. And the keeper of the prison awaking out of his sleep, and seeing the prison doors open, he drew out his sword, and would have killed himself, supposing that the prisoners had been fled.

"But Paul cried with a loud voice, saying, Do thyself no harm: for we are all here. Then he called for a light, and sprang in, and came trembling, and fell down before Paul and Silas, and brought them out, and said, Sirs, what must I do to be saved? And they said, Believe on the Lord Jesus Christ, and thou shalt be saved, and thy house. And they spake unto him the word of the Lord, and to all that were in his house.

"And he took them the same hour of the night, and washed their stripes; and was baptized, he and all his, straightway. And when he had brought them into his house, he set meat before them, and rejoiced, believing in God with all his house"—Acts 16:19-34

This is the fifth conversion to God, detailed for us in the book of Acts. First that of the Ethiopian eunuch—a black man; then of Saul of Tarsus—the Jew; next of Cornelius—the Gentile; in this chapter that of Lydia, whose heart the Lord opened—the first convert in Europe being a woman; and now that of this rough prison warden, suddenly changed from a heartless, cruel man into a humble follower of the lowly Jesus. The circumstances in connection with his salvation are precious and full of pertinent instruction.

The servants of God—Paul and Silas—were unceremoniously arrested, cruelly beaten, and then thrust into an underground dungeon. After putting many stripes upon them, the magistrates charged the jailor to keep the prisoners secure, apparently with the intention of treating them even more severely later on. This jailor shows his character by not just putting them into the inner prison, but thrusting them there. The inner prison

is said to have been a dark, damp, windowless, underground hole; there, in addition, in spite of their raw,
bleeding backs, they were put in the stocks. Those who
have seen pictures of the "pillory" in use some centuries
ago will know what stocks looked like, and can realize
the painful distress they caused to these messengers of
the Lord.

Yet, instead of groaning or complaining, or merely
suffering in silence, commiserating themselves upon
their wretched state, these preachers prayed and sang
praises to God; and at midnight, too—the darkest hour!
I guess the throbbing of their wounds did not permit
them to sleep, so they decided to wake up others and
not let them sleep either; they were successful, for we
read that the prisoners heard them. Paul and Silas
prayed, praised, and preached in prison. What a testimony to the triumphant grace of God! If midnight
stands for the darkest part of the night, it suggests that
true believers, even in the most distressful hours of their
experience, can yet sing praises to the Lord. It is easy
to be happy when everything goes well; but true spiritual power is apparent when the believer can sing in
hours of sorrow or pain. The other prisoners heard and
one may be sure that they marveled at the unwonted
sounds coming from the dungeon below.

God answered the faith and courage of His servants
in a most remarkable, startling way. There was a great
earthquake which rocked the foundations of the struc-
ture, broke open all the doors, and loosed every prisoner's chains off his hands and legs. Did you ever hear of

an earthquake that leaves a big building standing but only opens the doors; or one that makes chains fall off hands or legs? This peculiar earthquake was meant to impress upon these men that God was working; that God was speaking. It often takes a special earthquake to arouse sinners to their need; to wake them up to their fearful danger and the doom that lies ahead. Such moral earthquakes happen every day.

The earthquake shock aroused the turnkey from his sleep. Seeing the prison doors open and logically concluding that all the prisoners had used this golden opportunity to escape, he drew out his sword and was about to commit suicide when arrested by a loud voice, from the lips of his notable prisoner named Paul, who shouted: "Do thyself no harm: for we are all here." That cry brought the warden trembling to the feet of those he had treated so brutally the night before, and he cried, "Sirs, what must I do to be saved?" We do not read that the earthquake made this warden tremble, but the voice of Paul did. And it is no wonder, for Paul's cry contains three of the most startling, revolutionizing truths that the sinner must face, either here or hereafter:

1. It spoke of the "omniscience" of God. How did Paul know this wretched sinner was about to kill himself? That he did know is proven by the fact that he called to him to do himself no harm. Remember that it was midnight and pitch dark; that the apostles were in an underground dungeon where they could not possibly see anything or anyone. Yet they "saw" this man was about to plunge the sword into his heart. How

could they know this? Evidently the God whom they served had revealed the jailor's act to them. The jailor realized he had to do with a God who could see in the dark; a God who knows everything. The jailor learned he was face to face with Him who knew his every sin and wickedness. All sinners should remember this. They have to meet a God before whose eyes all things are naked and open. It is impossible to hide one's sins from Him; He knows. He can see in the dark.

2. Paul's cry spoke of the "omnipotence" of God. Paul cried: "We are all here." Imagine a prison, full of men awaiting trial for their crimes and many perhaps waiting for the day of execution; all their chains had dropped off; all the prison doors were open. Yet Paul assures the jailor not one of them had run away. Not one of them had used this golden opportunity for freedom. There is only one explanation for this. The same God who knows everything is also the God who holds everything. The same God who loosed all the chains and blasted all the doors open, who had used His power to do this, now employed that same power to keep those prisoners from escaping. What a God! Yes, that wicked man learned that night what every sinner needs to learn —that God is a God of Almighty power. None can withstand Him and escape. He will keep sinners in hell forever, and it will not require locked doors or handcuffs either.

3. Then, most blessed, the jailor learned that this God is a God of wondrous love. "Do thyself no harm" told him so. He found out that the God whose servants he

had so abused, loved him better than he loved himself. He was about to commit suicide—to rob himself forever of a chance for divine mercy, or a chance to escape the damnation of hell. But this God he knew not hitherto had stopped him. Yes indeed, God's love is boundless; love told out to the full in the Cross of our Saviour Jesus Christ.

No wonder he came in trembling. Many a sinner has since come trembling to the feet of Jesus, marveling at the grace offered to him through the undeserved grace of God. This sinner called for a light; when a soul is aroused from the sleep of death, the first thing wanted is "light."

"What must I do to be saved?" To a soul evidently under conviction of sin, the precious ready reply is: "Believe on the Lord Jesus Christ, and thou shalt be saved." I am sure that all the emphasis should be placed on the words, "the Lord Jesus Christ"; not on the *believing*. You can believe anything or anyone, but that will not save the soul. Only *He* can save. This man was not told to go and *do* something in order to be saved, but to look to Him who has done it all; to look to Jesus.

The promise of salvation was not only to him but to all that were in his house. The amazing conversion of the father apparently made the family ready and eager to listen to the message of salvation, too; and how Paul and Silas would delight to tell the sweet story of Jesus and His love to all of them. All of them believed and rejoiced and were baptized as an expression of their faith in the Son of God, of whom probably that night they heard for the first time.

Further, the jailor showed the reality of his conversion by the instant change in his conduct. He brought Paul and Silas out of the dungeon, washed their wounds, brought them into his house, and made them a feast—all sure proofs of the reality of his new birth; evidences of a new nature bearing fruit for God. It is to me intensely interesting to note that Paul preached first to this family, before anything else was done. The washing of their wounds, the needed food, etc., all had to wait while the story of God's love was told to this troubled soul. What amazing self-abnegation this depicts!

And now one wonders what reaction was produced in the prisoners who were, if not witnesses, at least auditors of all this. Their bonds were loosed; the doors were open; the light shone in the prison; they could hear and probably see all that went on; and they were present at that wonderful meeting, for, as we saw, none had fled. They might, as the jailor did, have fallen down at Paul's feet and called for mercy to the God who had so wondrously displayed His power and glory. Did they? The Bible leaves the answer unsaid. No doubt the chains were put on again, the doors were secured, and the preachers of the gospel went out, leaving the sadness and darkness of prison life behind.

So today, how many there are who listen to the praying, praising, and preaching that goes on all around them; but it leaves them unmoved. How many have been brought up in Christian homes; have heard the good news all their lives; yet turn away from it untouched. These servants of Christ were there for a little while, and then they left. So the ministers of the gospel are in this world, which is truly a prison to the redeemed soul. By-and-by they will leave to go home to Heaven; and for the prisoners of sin left behind there remains the eternal darkness, sorrow, and regret. How is it with *you*, who read these lines? Now anyone may come to Christ, as these prisoners might have come to Paul and Silas. But someday, when the day of grace is over, the chains will bind irrevocably those who turn away. Oh, "believe on the Lord Jesus Christ, and thou shalt be saved."

34

"Who Are Ye?"

"THEN CERTAIN of the vagabond Jews, exorcists, took upon them to call over them which had evil spirits the name of the Lord Jesus, saying, We adjure you by Jesus whom Paul preacheth. And there were seven sons of one Sceva, a Jew, and chief of the priests, which did so. And the evil spirit answered and said, Jesus I know, and Paul I know; but *who are ye?*

"And the man in whom the evil spirit was leaped on them, and overcame them, and prevailed against them, so that they fled out of that house naked and wounded. And this was known to all the Jews and Greeks also dwelling at Ephesus; and fear fell on them all, and the name of the Lord was magnified."—Acts 19:13-17

Acts 19 records Paul's long stay in Ephesus, with its many interesting experiences. We are told in verse 10 that all in Asia, both Jews and Greeks, heard the word of the Lord Jesus. The Word of God mightily grew and prevailed, as we learn from verse 20. More miracles were done by Paul here than perhaps anywhere else.

Wherever God works, Satan also is busy. Some of Satan's tools, from the very family of the priests, sought to cast out evil spirits in imitation of the servants of the Lord and of the Lord Himself. The striking thing is that

God would not let them succeed, and used another tool of Satan to oppose the first. We have a picture of Satan fighting himself; it is not believers alone who often fight each other instead of fighting the common enemy. It is rather refreshing to find in our text that the devil is not much wiser either, for it is exactly what he does in this incident. On the other hand, perhaps Satan does things like these on purpose, for he loves to confuse the issue, as the fearful confusion in religious thought so clearly proves.

These exorcists tried to cast out evil spirits by using the Name of Jesus, whom Paul preached; and the man with the evil spirit answered, "Jesus I know, and Paul I know." Both exorcists and the evil spirit omit Christ's title of "Lord"; which is a common practice among those who are not true to Christ. It behooves believers to call Him Lord, for it is with the mouth that we confess Jesus as Lord. Again we read that "no man can say that Jesus is the Lord but by the Holy Ghost" (1 Corinthians 12:3).

The evil spirit answered in these startling words: "Jesus I know, and Paul I know; but who are ye?" It is an evil, satanic spirit, who said, "Jesus I know." But, as a matter of fact, he did *not* know Jesus, for to really know Jesus is to have life eternal (John 17:3). How many sinners claim to know the Lord when in reality they do not know Him at all; how many take the Name of Jesus on their lips who are complete strangers to Him in their hearts! You may say you know Jesus, but the

question is: Does *He* know you? To many in that day
He shall say, "Depart, I know you not." But it is a great
joy indeed to be able to say truthfully, "Jesus I know."
If that is the case, you will gladly acknowledge Him
Lord and surrender your life to Him, like Paul, who
counted all things but loss for the excellency of the
knowledge of Christ Jesus his Lord.

These exorcists used the Name of Jesus, yet when
set upon by the man possessed of the evil spirit, they
were overcome and fled out of the house naked and
wounded. Those who know Jesus only by profession,
and not in true living faith, are defeated; but those who
truly know and love Him always gain the victory
through Christ. These fled naked and wounded, but the
Christian stands, instead of fleeing; he is clothed in the
best robe of righteousness and with the armor of God,
instead of being naked. Instead of being overcome, he is
more than conqueror through Him that loves us. Praise
His Name!

The evil spirit said: "Jesus I know, and Paul I know."
Those two are indeed worth knowing. "But who are
ye?" Satan tells us here, by the mouth of this evil spirit,
that he does not care to know the lesser lights, even
though they were some of his own dupes. It seems that
the devil is a snob. How unlike our blessed Lord, whose
heart goes out to the most insignificant and humblest of
His saints. The Lord knoweth them that are His; He
loves all His own with an eternal love. But Satan cares
to know only the aristocracy; he does not hobnob with

sinners. He does not care to keep company with the common sinner, yet will spend eternity with sinners of the deepest dye.

The evil spirit knew Jesus and Paul and was willing to own acquaintance with them. "But who are *ye?*" Satan had only contempt for this small fry. I wonder whether the devil would admit knowing me? Would he want to say of me as of these: "Who are you? I never heard of you." The Bible indicates that Satan does not pay any particular attention to many of God's people. It shows he specially notices the worth-while among God's saints. All the "great" men in Scripture were the objects of the devil's notice and animosity. It is truly an honor when Satan cares to know you.

Satan said, as it were: "Job I know." The devil's reply to the Lord in Job 1:9-12 shows he had well considered Job and knew that he was an outstanding character; one whose fall would be a real victory for Satan.

Satan said, as it were: "Peter I know." Said the Lord to Peter: "Satan hath desired to have you, that he may sift you as wheat: but I have prayed for thee, that thy faith fail not" (Luke 22:31-32). Peter was an aggressive, forthright follower of Christ and the devil felt that if he could get him to fall, it would be a most important victory for him and a defeat for the Lord Jesus.

Satan said, as it were: "Paul I know. I'll get him discouraged and I'll make him give up his militant service for Christ." And so God permitted Satan to afflict Paul with some physical irritation—a thorn in the flesh, the messenger of Satan to buffet him (2 Corinthians 12:7).

And what can we say concerning the devil's acknowledgment of the greatness of our glorious Lord? Truly he said of Him: "Jesus I know." No one was ever harassed and persecuted and tried by Satan like our adorable Lord, but He could triumphantly say to him twice over: "Get thee behind Me, Satan." Once at the beginning of His public ministry when Satan sought to turn Him from the Cross by dangling before Him the glory of this world; then again at the end when he sought to dissuade Him by reminding Him of the shame of the cross (Matthew 16:22-23).

In all these cases, and in many more, Satan was defeated. In our text he made his own emissaries run, but he can't make the Lord Jesus or His servants run; these were all made only the more outstandingly useful through their experience at the devil's hands.

Yes, Satan knows Jesus, Peter, Paul. Does he know *me?* I would hate to live so that even the devil would not be anxious to acknowledge acquaintance with me. As one has well said: if you never want to be bothered by the devil, just do nothing, say nothing, be nothing.

As a result of all this, the Name of the Lord Jesus was magnified (verse 17). The devil's defeat and the believer's victory alike bring glory to the Name of Him under whose banner we fight the fight of faith.

35

Eutychus Fell Down

"AND WE sailed away from Philippi after the days of unleavened bread, and came unto them to Troas in five days; where we abode seven days. And upon the first day of the week, when the disciples came together to break bread, Paul preached unto them, ready to depart on the morrow; and continued his speech until midnight. And there were many lights in the upper chamber, where they were gathered together.

"And there sat in a window a certain young man named Eutychus, being fallen into a deep sleep; and as Paul was long preaching, he sunk down with sleep, and fell down from the third loft, and was taken up dead.

"And Paul went down, and fell on him, and embracing him said, Trouble not yourselves; for his life is in him." When he therefore was come up again, and had broken bread, and eaten, and talked a long while, even till break of day, so he departed. And they brought the young man alive, and were not a little comforted"—Acts 20:6-12

This unique experience during Paul's travels is one of my pet subjects, on which I love to speak. It is full of practical instruction, and presented in a graphic, pictorial manner. Let us look at it in detail:

Paul is on his way to Jerusalem, on that final journey that eventually ended in his martyrdom in Rome. On the way they stopped off at Troas (the Troy of Greek history), and arrived there on a Monday; for we are told they remained there seven days and left the morning after the first day of the week, the day on which Eutychus' fall occurred.

Please notice that Paul stayed at Troas for a full week, apparently to be with these saints on Lord's day for the breaking of bread with them. It seems to me this shows how precious the remembrance feast was to him, specially when he was so anxious to get down to Jerusalem that he would not even stop at Ephesus (verse 16). Is the remembrance of the Lord precious to you? It is *the* expression of Christian unity and fellowship on earth —the only physical, visible evidence of the oneness of believers, and of course also of the infinite worth of the death of our Lord at Calvary.

Next, notice that they met on the first day of the week, when the disciples came together to break bread. The language indicates that it was their custom to meet every Lord's day for this happy and holy occasion; it furnishes strong proof the early disciples understood it was the Lord's desire that His people should celebrate His death in this way at least once a week.

Then, there were many lights in the chamber where they met. These should tell us that, when saints meet, there are truly many lights present in a spiritual sense. There is the light of God's precious Word; the light of the Holy Spirit cast upon the pages of the Word illuminating it for us, for He is called the Spirit of "Light"; there is the light each individual believer sheds, for we all shine as lights in the world. Truly the upper chamber is well lit; we believers live truly in a blaze of glory. They met at night. Down below was darkness, but up above it was light. Even so, this world lies in the darkness of sin and unbelief, while the saints enjoy the light of God's presence and of His Word. It was so in Egypt long ago; there was one mighty difference those three days of thick darkness. It was dark all over the land, but the children of Israel had light in their dwellings; in Egypt it was dark inside and outside, but in Israel there was bright light within.

These in Acts 20 met in an upper room, three stories above the ground, for we read that Eutychus fell down from the third loft. The number three in Scripture stands for the deity, as well as for the death and the third-day resurrection of Christ. So in this picture we see these believers, as it were, above the level of the world; separated by the death and resurrection of their Lord from the sinful world around; elevated that much above the world's level.

Paul preached unto them; thus they enjoyed the ministry of this chosen vessel, to whom had been committed the unfolding of truth concerning the Church—the heavenly character of its blessings and destiny. It is the ministry in Scripture that tells us we are not of this world, that bids us to set our mind on things above, where Christ sitteth at the right hand of God. Notice how richly these saints were blessed, as we are in this day of Christian grace.

They had at least five great privileges to enjoy:

1. There was the fellowship of saints; for they came together.

2. They had the privilege of remembering the Lord in His precious death.

3. They met in a blaze of light; for all believers are in the light.

4. They were in spiritual elevation above the low level of the world.

5. They had the wonderful New Testament ministry, of which the apostle is the great exponent in the Scriptures.

Thus they were truly "well off," which is always a danger, whether in the material or spiritual realm. Prosperity is very apt to lead to self-confidence and spiritual carelessness. This is illustrated in the story of this young man Eutychus who fell out of the window, for his very name means just that: "Well off." When believers are well off, they are apt to fall, as this young man did.

Eutychus was sitting in a window, which is a very dangerous spot to be in, specially when this window is on the third floor. Someone should have pulled him to safer territory ere he fell. When a believer is sitting in a window—which means that he is neither in the room nor out—he is in serious danger. A Christian should be out-and-out for Christ, and in-and-in with the saints. A young man sitting in the window on the third floor is afflicted with too big a dose of self-confidence, and self-confidence is always misplaced confidence, as this fellow shortly was to find out. When Peter said, "Though all shall deny Thee, yet will not I," he had already fallen, though he wist it not. Elders should be on the alert for young believers afflicted with self-conceit, for they are headed for a fall. Better take them in before they become down-and-out.

Why was Eutychus sitting in the window anyway? Why not sit with his brothers and sisters? Could it be he was at loggerheads with them? Often when believers begin to sit further and further to the rear of the meeting place, we may see an indication of spiritual departure; the time to go after them in love is then, not later. Elder brethren, with hearts of love for the saints, should watch for any indication of creeping coldness and spiritual paralysis.

Perhaps Eutychus had not been coming regularly to the meetings, but, having heard of the coming of this famous apostle, he made it a point to be there that night. We have many of those sermon-tasters among us. They come to services only on special occasions. They tell you they don't come regularly because they *get* so little out of the ordinary prayer meeting or Bible study. They have the wrong psychology; the Scripture teaches that we should come to meet with the saints not to get but to *give*. Eutychus may have come to hear Paul preach and not finding him so very interesting after all, he fell asleep. (It gives me a sort of sneaky satisfaction to find that at least one person went to sleep under Paul's preaching; I don't feel so badly now when they do it under mine.) Eutychus may have learned the hard way that it is not the preacher that makes the Word precious, but the condition of soul of the hearer. If you have a soul for the food you will get food for your soul.

All of a sudden Paul's sermon is interrupted by a crashing fall. Eutychus fell out of the window all the way down to the ground floor—three stories down.

But, before he fell, he had fallen already. His fall from the window was not a sudden affair. Verse 9 tells us that he had fallen long before he fell. He had fallen *into* a deep sleep before he fell *out of* the window. The first fall was not as spectacular as the second, but it was by far the more fatal. The second fall resulted in his blessing; the first in his grief and pain. It tells us the story that—spiritually speaking—no believer ever falls *suddenly*.

Perhaps a saint falls into some terrible moral sin; others marvel at it and say, "I just can't believe it." But if you could have seen what God sees, you would have seen that the seed of that collapse had been planted long before. There is no such thing as falling into sin; the soul walks into it, rather, oftentimes over a period of years; and then suddenly the inward rot breaks out into outward corruption.

Take David as a sample. We all know his sad sin in connection with Bathsheba. This did not happen overnight. The kings of Israel were told they were not to multiply wives to themselves (Deuteronomy 17:17); they were to have only one wife each. Yet David had married one woman after another in clear defiance of God's written Word. He had yielded to his passion for women—done it within the limits of the law by legally marrying them; but the time came when this desire led him astray, and we know how he suffered for it all the rest of his life.

Eutychus fell all the way from the third-floor separation from the world and its spiritual darkness down to its sad level, all the way from the top to the bottom. How many of us, before or since, have done so too. Peter at one moment said, "Thou art the Christ, the Son of the living God"; and not long after, with curses and oaths, swore saying, "I know not the man of whom ye speak." Can it be possible? Yes, it is; with Simon Peter and with you and me, too. Remember this: the Scripture teaches that the flesh in the believer is no better than in the unbeliever. The flesh never improves; it must be kept under as the believer walks with God in humility, daily dependence, and unsparing self-judgment.

Now Paul went down and fell on this fallen young man. Isn't this amazing? Eutychus fell all the way from the third floor to the bottom, and now Paul falls on him some more. You'd think he had had enough, and that Paul was only adding insult to injury. But please note that Paul *went down first*, before he fell on him. He did not fall on this foolish young man from his own superior elevation on the third floor, but he went down to the young man's level and then fell on him.

What a lovely picture this is of the ministry of a true pastor. If we are to be a help to a fallen believer and be used to his restoration, we must not fall on him from our height, but go down to his level. If we fall on him from the third floor we are apt to knock the last bit of breath out of him, if there is any left; and injure not only the fallen one but ourself as well. When a Christian sins, some jump on him from their exalted spiritual superiority and perhaps they say: "You should not have done it; I would never do a thing like that; you ought to get all that is coming to you." No, God's Word tells us to restore the fallen one "in the spirit of meekness; considering thyself, lest thou also be tempted." In other words, to do as Paul did: go down to the level of the fallen one, and in tenderness seek in humility and self-judgment to bring him back to communion with the Lord.

That is what Paul did. He went down; then fell on him; then embraced him. Note these three great steps. First come to the fallen one in humility and self-abnegation; then (by falling on him) do tell him seriously and plainly of the awful dishonor he has brought on the Name of Christ; then—embrace him; that is, in love seek to win him back to the One against whom he has sinned. Paul pressed this young man to his own beating heart of love and compassion. That word "embraced" is a very strong word, suggesting that he fervently pressed him to his bosom. Ah, love is a strong cord that will bind the weakest, most sinful one.

Paul said: "His life is in him." It is not clear from the text whether this means that the fall had killed him or that he was merely restored from the shock and result of the fall. When the Word of God leaves the language rather ambiguous it is often intended to be so. If the fall had killed him, it would in its spiritual meaning suggest that the young man represents an unbeliever—one who has no divine life. Sinners often fall into serious sin which may lead to their conversion, through the mercy of God. If the young man had not died from the fall, it would indicate, I believe, that he represents a believer, for no matter how serious a fall a believer may sustain, he cannot by it lose his salvation. Such need restoration; need to confess their sins to be restored to communion with God and with His saints. In either case, the ministry performed by Paul has its message for every shepherd of the sheep. We should seek the salvation of the lost and the restoration of the saved. Love will accomplish so much in either case.

After the excitement Paul continued preaching for a long time, till break of day. Just because Eutychus fell down, Paul did not take the blame for it because of his lengthy sermon, but kept on. One would love to see sermons nowadays interrupted by some such sensational incident—the recovery of fallen saints or the conversion of lost sinners.

36

Paul's Address to the Elders of Ephesus

"AND FROM Miletus he sent to Ephesus, and called the elders of the church. And when they were come to him, he said unto them, Ye know, from the first day that I came into Asia, after what manner I have been with you at all seasons, Serving the Lord with all humility of mind, and with many tears, and temptations, which befell me by the lying in wait of the Jews: and how I kept back nothing that was profitable unto you, but have shewed you, and have taught you publickly, and from house to house, testifying both to the Jews, and also to the Greeks, repentance toward God, and faith toward our Lord Jesus Christ.

"And now, behold, I go bound in the spirit unto Jerusalem, not knowing the things that shall befall me there: save that the Holy Ghost witnesseth in every city, saying that bonds and afflictions abide me. But none of these things move me, neither count I my life dear unto myself, so that I might finish my course with joy, and the ministry, which I have received of the Lord Jesus, to testify the gospel of the grace of God.

"And now, behold, I know that ye all, among whom I have gone preaching the kingdom of God, shall see my face no more. Wherefore I take you to record this day, that I am pure from the blood of all men. For I have not shunned to declare unto you all the counsel of God.

"Take heed therefore unto yourselves, and to all the flock, over the which the Holy Ghost hath made you overseers, to feed the church of God, which He hath purchased with His own blood. For I know this, that after my departing shall grievous wolves enter in among you, not sparing the flock. Also of your own selves shall men arise, speaking perverse things, to draw away disciples after them.

"Therefore watch, and remember, that by the space of three years I ceased not to warn every one night and day with tears. And now, brethren, I commend you to God, and to the word of His grace, which is able to build you up, and to give you an inheritance among all them which are sanctified. I have coveted no man's silver, or gold, or apparel. Yea, ye yourselves know, that these hands have ministered unto my necessities, and to them that were with me.

"I have shewed you all things, how that so labouring ye ought to support the weak, and to remember the words of the Lord Jesus, how He said, It is more blessed to give than to receive.

"And when he had thus spoken, he kneeled down, and prayed with them all. And they all wept sore, and fell on Paul's neck, and kissed him, Sorrowing most of all for the words which he spake, that they should see his face no more. And they accompanied him unto the ship"—Acts 20:17-38

In this chapter we reach the end of Paul's ministry as recorded, since from here on he becomes a prisoner of the Lord and eventually His martyr. His missionary zeal in going to the regions beyond is approaching its climax and the verses now before us contain a matchless summation of his labors of the *past* years; his *present* advice and warning; and the *future* prospect and its testimony for Christ. The whole portion is a beautiful comment on the man, his methods, ministry, message, manner of life, meekness of mind, and modesty. It is the voice of one who was not only an evangelist entrusted with the gospel of God's grace, but also a teacher par excellence, and a true pastor of the flock. This valedictory address is truly a marvelous expression of the ideal Christian ministry and has the highest possible value for every earnest Christian who seeks to serve the Lord after the great example of the apostle to the Gentiles.

Paul calls for the elders of the church of Ephesus. Not the elders of Corinth, or of Galatia, but of Ephesus, where the full truth as to the Church and its heavenly character was taught—as it is in the Epistle to the Ephesians so clearly expounded. Paul's farewell address is God's Word for His Church today.

Paul contemplates no apostolic succession, as some falsely claim today. The only apostolic succession he knows of is that of grievous wolves entering in, not sparing the flock. How fully that prediction has come to pass, all Church history bears witness. From among themselves would men arise speaking perverse things, drawing away disciples after them. Paul warns of evil coming from within as well as from without. There were to be no successors to the apostles, but the Lord would raise up elders in the assemblies of the saints, to take on themselves the care of the Lord's people. To them Paul leaves his last words of advice and warning, and presents his own sacrificial life as a sample of true Christian devotion.

Note these features in the make-up of the true minister of Christ:

1. He served the Lord with all humility of mind (verse 19). The first and foremost quality in a preacher should be humility. Nothing is more contemptible than spiritual conceit and pride. The servant of Christ should be clothed (girded) with humility.

2. He served with many tears (verse 19). For three years he warned everyone night and day with tears (verse 31). The sower is to go forth weeping, bearing precious seed, watering the Word with his tears and prayers. Lost sinners and needy saints ever call for the deepest exercise of soul on the part of the true pastor.

3. Paul kept back nothing that was profitable (verse 20). He had not shunned declaring unto them all the counsel of God (verse 27). He was no timeserver; he did not seek to please men, and so he was pure from the blood of all men. As a faithful servant he did not always come in the spirit of meekness, but sometimes had to use the rod (1 Corinthians 4:21).

4. He taught the truth publicly and from house to house. Not only from the platform, but in personal contact with individuals he preached Christ. Oftentimes the

personal touch is far more effective than any other type
or method in reaching souls.

5. He was not in the Lord's work for the sake of
money (verse 33). He does teach that it is right that the
minister of the Word should be supported, for they that
preach the gospel should live of the gospel. But it is
wrong to pretend the service of the Lord for the sake
of material gain; yet how often is the Name of Christ dis-
honored by greedy self-seeking interest.

6. Instead of looking for money, Paul had worked
with his own hands and supported not only himself but
also those with him (verses 34-35). Many can serve the
Lord effectively and at the same time earn their own
living. Paul bids the elders to remember the words of
the Lord Jesus that it is "more blessed to give than to
receive." Such words are not recorded anywhere in any
of the Gospels, but their sentiment was embodied in our
Lord's preaching and practising. Perhaps He did say
those very words; they are certainly worth remembering at all times.

7. Paul's whole life had been one of total self-abnegation. He did not count his life dear to himself (verse 24),
so that he might finish his course with joy. He did not
count his life dear to himself; he counted it dear to his
Lord. A life, unless lived for Christ, is really not worth
anything. No need to set a high value on it. But, when
lived for Him, it is indeed priceless and then it is perfectly safe to leave it in His hands. He knows how,
where, when, and how long to use it. One can afford to
be "reckless" with his life when it has been committed
to Him.

8. No one perhaps ever knew such trials, suffering, and dishonor as did Paul, but it did not make him cynical. He says that he wanted to finish his course with joy (verse 24). He knew much of sorrow, yet he was always rejoicing. So like his Master, who for the joy set before Him endured the Cross, despising the shame; who could say, with the Cross and all its awful horror before Him: "I delight to do Thy will, O God." The Christian's service should not be one of cold duty, but of a warm, loving, joyous response.

9. Paul preached a fourfold message as suggested in this address:

> repentance toward God and faith toward our Lord Jesus Christ (verse 21);
> the gospel of the grace of God (verse 24);
> the kingdom of God (verse 25);
> the whole counsel of God (verse 27).

It seems to me that in these four types of ministry the first and third stress the truth of the believer's responsibility: first of all to repent and believe the gospel as a sinner; then to be obedient as a subject in His kingdom—to be counted worthy of the kingdom of God, for which we also suffer (2 Thessalonians 1:5).

The other two, the second and fourth, present God's sovereign grace: first, the gospel of His matchless love preached to lost sinners, and then the whole revelation of divine truth so fully developed in the Christian Epistles. Thus Paul's varied ministry completely covered every phase of gospel and Christian teaching.

And now this aged servant of the Lord, about to leave those dear saints forever, commits them to God and to the Word of His grace. He does not commit them to popes or priests, to lords or laymen, but to God—to the God who has revealed Himself as a God of grace. To God who is quite able to make the feeblest of His people understand His Word, for every believer has received the Spirit of God that he might know the things freely given to him of God (1 Corinthians 2:12).

Paul reminds these Ephesian elders that the Holy Spirit had made them overseers (the same word is translated *bishops*, as in Philippians 1:1 and elsewhere). Though we read in Acts that Paul had appointed these men to their service as elders, yet he tells them it had been done under the guidance and by the authority of the Spirit of God. While the Lord Jesus is the only Head of the Church that the Bible recognizes, He sees fit to raise up, in each assembly of His saints, human leaders called elders—as to their age; and overseers or bishops —as to their qualification. Scripture makes no provision for the appointment of elders after Paul's departure, but it does show that those who are fitted by God to lead and guide the saints should be recognized and esteemed highly for their works' sake (1 Thessalonians 5:12-13).

These elders are told, first of all, to take heed to "themselves." Paul tells Timothy the same thing (1 Timothy 4:16) where we read: "Take heed unto thyself." Leaders among the Lord's people should see to it that their own lives are consistent so that they be godly, grave, and gracious. Read the qualifications of an elder in 1 Timothy 3:1-7.

Secondly, they should look after the flock. Peter, himself an elder, tells us the same thing in 1 Peter 5:1-5. The flock, says Peter, is the flock of God (sometimes ministers talk about "my" flock, but it is not theirs); often preachers fleece the flock rather than feed it. Both in Acts 20 and in 1 Peter 5 the Greek word translated *feed* is the word *shepherd*. The people of God of course need food, and it is a great privilege to lead the sheep to green pastures; but they specially need pastoral care and wise leadership.

The Authorized Version reads that the Holy Spirit had made these elders overseers *over* the flock, but the Greek word means rather *among*, as it is correctly given in 1 Peter 5:2. Elders are not given a place as lords, but of leaders; not over, but amidst the flock. They are part of and with the saints, leading them not by virtue of conferred authority, but by spiritual example and divinely-given ability. Such shepherds are directly responsible to the "Chief" Shepherd, and at that day shall receive the crown of glory from His hands. It is to our Lord a very precious ministry; His blood-bought saints are very dear to Him.

Following Paul's example these elders were to:

Take heed to themselves; shepherd the flock; watch over them and warn them. Blessed is the church that has earnest, consecrated elders to lead the believers to green pastures and beside the still waters, as well as to protect the lambs from the ravening wolf.

37

"I Verily Thought With Myself"

"I verily thought with myself, that I ought to do many things contrary to the name of Jesus of Nazareth."—Acts 26:9

I would like to devote a little space to this unique confession of the erstwhile persecutor of the saints as he rehearses before King Agrippa his sensational experience. There are at least seven interesting points in this remarkable verse:

1. *I*—the wrong person filled his vision. What an enemy this "I" is to the natural man! It is a great relief when it is crucified with Christ; when true deliverance and peace are known; when it is no longer I, but Christ who dwells in me, that sits on the throne of my heart.

2. I verily *thought*—and he thought wrong. How man prides himself on his intellectual capacity, not knowing, it seems, what the Scriptures teach so clearly: that God's thoughts are higher than our thoughts as the heavens are higher than the earth. God has given a revelation—the Scriptures of truth—to guide our thinking, to set and keep our thoughts in the right channels. Every thought must be brought into captivity to the obedience of Christ (2 Corinthians 10:5).

3. I thought *with myself*. What a tragedy looms in

this unique expression of opinionated self-sufficiency. It reminds one of the story our Lord told about the farmer whose barns were bursting with crops and who thought "within himself" saying, "What shall I do?" It is like the Pharisee of Luke 18 who prayed "with himself." None of these sought counsel elsewhere; they knew it all; they left God out of their reckoning. In prayer we seek counsel from God, but Saul never really asked advice from the God he professed to serve. His very thoughts did not leave home. The most narrow-minded person is the one who leaves God out; whose thoughts never leave the narrow confines of his own limited brain. Depend upon it, the soul that does not seek help from the God of omniscience and omnipotence will inevitably go wrong somewhere. Saul found it so. Thinking, in his fanatical zeal, that he did God's will, he was actually doing the exact reverse.

4. I *ought to*. Duty was Saul of Tarsus' motive prior to his conversion. Duty is but a cold, often heartless motive. Duty fails to render the heart to God, who says, "Son, give Me thine heart!" The commandments did not say first "thou shalt serve the Lord thy God," but "thou shalt *love* the Lord thy God with all thine heart." The elder son said to his father, "Lo, these many years do I serve thee," but it had made him only hard and bitter and censorious when his sinful but repentant prodigal brother was welcomed home. A life ordered by duty can be very hard, cold, and Pharasaic. The worst madman is a religious one; in others the conscience is a restraining force; in him it becomes a relent-

lessly compelling one. Conscience made Saul a murderer of Christians; love, the mighty love of Christ, made him a humble follower of the Lord Jesus Christ and a suffering servant of his Lord. It is the love of Christ—not hard duty—that is to constrain the believer henceforth not to live unto himself but unto Him who died for him and rose again.

5. I ought to *do*. Man loves to do. With God, to "be" comes first. Service from a sinner is not acceptable to Him. Worship precedes service. The heart must be right with God before the hands are fit to do His will. We do not become His by good works, but, once saved, we are created in Christ unto good works; works that flow from a heart filled with the wonder of the love of Christ.

6. *Many things*. But, as the Lord said of Mary in Luke 10, *"One* thing is needful." As Paul writes in Philippians 3:13: "This one thing I do"; I press toward the mark, forgetting the things behind. The young ruler of Mark 10 did many things too, but the Saviour told him that he lacked *one* thing—the one thing necessary. Without saving faith in Christ, which produces the love of God in the soul, no works, no matter how many or how great, are worth anything in His sight; in fact, they are sins that need to be repented of.

7. *Contrary to the Name of Jesus of Nazareth*. Saul of Tarsus did not know Jesus; that was the evil root from which sprang all his evil course. He learned to know and love Him later, and his whole life became revolutionized. From a persecutor he became the per-

secuted; hard duty became transmuted into loving, lowly service. Jesus' Name, which once he despised, now became his boast and glory. He learned that the despised Jesus of Nazareth was actually the Lord of glory, for at his conversion he saw Him in the opened Heaven seated at the right hand of God. Henceforth he gloried in the Cross of Christ, by which the world was crucified unto him and he to the world.

38

King Agrippa Hears the Gospel

"WHEREUPON as I went to Damacus with authority and commission from the chief priests, at midday, O king, I saw in the way a light from heaven, above the brightness of the sun, shining round about me and them which journeyed with me. And when we were all fallen to the earth, I heard a voice speaking unto me, and saying in the Hebrew tongue, Saul, Saul, why persecutest thou Me? it is hard for thee to kick against the pricks. And I said, Who art Thou, Lord?

"And He said, I am Jesus whom thou persecutest. But rise, and stand upon thy feet: for I have appeared unto thee for this purpose, to make thee a minister and a witness both of these things which thou hast seen, and of those things in the which I will appear unto thee;

"Delivering thee from the people, and from the Gentiles, unto whom now I send thee, to open their eyes, and to turn them from darkness to light, and from the power of Satan unto God, that they may receive forgiveness of sins, and inheritance among them which are sanctified by faith that is in Me"—Acts 26:12-18

Speaking of his conversion before King Agrippa, Paul mentions "a vision and a voice." Paul saw a light above the brightness of the sun. He tells us on another occa-

sion that he saw the Lord at this time. At Creation God
commanded the light to shine out of darkness (2 Corinthians 4:6), as the light of the sun later on was seen in
its glory. But a light far brighter—the light of the
knowledge of the glory of God in the face of Jesus
Christ shines into the darkened heart when God meets
the sinner, as here He met Paul. The glorious light Paul
saw, and which smote him blind, is the light we see in a
spiritual way when we see Christ as our Saviour. Paul
saw a light from Heaven and ever after his ministry was
marked by that heavenly glow.

Then he heard a voice—the voice of the Lord Jesus.
A voice that called him by name and that sent him forth
to preach Christ to the world. In a different way—
through the Word by the Spirit—that same voice calls
us and sends us forth with the gospel also.

The Lord said to Paul that He appeared to him to
make him a minister and a witness, delivering him from
the people (of Israel) and from the Gentiles, unto whom
now He sent him. That word *deliver* means to *take up*
or *take out;* the thought seems to be that Paul henceforth
would be no longer a Jew and certainly not a Gentile,
but he would be taken out from both and belong to this
new Body—the Church—which is neither Jew nor Gentile, though composed of both classes, but those saved
by God's grace.

Paul's eyes were first closed to his awful past, then
opened to see Christ in His glory; and now he is sent out
to "open the eyes" of others and to turn them from darkness to light and from the power of Satan unto God.

Paul says he had a threefold message to proclaim, with three negative blessings and three positive ones.

The negative ones are:

1. To turn men from darkness, from the moral darkness in which the sinner lives and moves.

2. To turn men from the power of Satan. From sin and from Satan, from the guilt and from the power of sin.

3. To receive forgiveness of sins. All the deeds of the past wiped away forever, for the blood of Jesus cleanseth from all sin.

The three positive blessings:

4. To turn men to light. As Peter says: "God has called us out of darkness into His marvelous light." And in that light of life we'll walk till traveling days are done.

5. To turn from the power of Satan *unto God*. How wonderful is deliverance from the sinister domination of the devil into the liberty of grace wherewith Christ sets us free. God has not only saved us, but now by His Spirit lives in us, to will as well as to do His good pleasure.

6. To assure the believer of a heavenly inheritance, which we already now may enjoy in large measure as God has put within us the "earnest" of His Spirit (Ephesians 1:14).

In these three positive blessings the believer in Jesus is lifted into a new position; he receives a new power and faces a new prospect.

King Agrippa, what do you have to say about all this? What do you have in comparison that is worth having? You with your earthly power, your greed, and your lust. Says Paul to him, "I would to God, that not only thou, but also all that hear me this day, were both almost, and altogether such as I am, except these bonds." The prisoner was far happier than the king. So is every believer in Jesus—no matter how humble his station in life.

39

The Serpent and the Fire

"AND WHEN they were escaped, then they knew that the island was called Melita. And the barbarous people shewed us no little kindness: for they kindled a fire, and received us every one, because of the present rain, and because of the cold.

"And when Paul had gathered a bundle of sticks, and laid them on the fire, there came a viper out of the heat, and fastened on his hand. And when the barbarians saw the venomous beast hang on his hand, they said among themselves, No doubt this man is a murderer, whom, though he hath escaped the sea, yet vengeance suffereth not to live. And he shook off the beast into the fire, and felt no harm.

"Howbeit, they looked when he should have swollen, or fallen down dead suddenly: but after they had looked a great while, and saw no harm come to him, they changed their minds, and said that he was a god"—Acts 28:1-6

There are some helpful lessons to be learned from this appealing sidelight on Paul's experiences.

Because of the rain and the cold a fire had been kindled. The barbarous people did it, we are told. Oftentimes sinners can be more kind in acts of thoughtfulness than Christians are. As these needed warmth for their bodies, we need it for our souls. Believers so readily get cold in a spiritual way; they need fire to keep warm and zealous in the cause of Christ and the enjoyment of His Word. Various means of keeping warm are suggested in the Bible. One very important one is, of course, by having the heart warmed with the precious truth of the Word. As the Psalmist says, "While I was musing the fire burned" (Psalm 39:3). There is a tremendous need for meditation on God's Word, so that the Lord and His Word may be precious to us. Another thing that keeps us warm is jealousy for the honor of our Lord, for we are told in Song of Solomon 8:6 that jealousy has a most vehement flame.

One of the best ways to keep warm is to meet with fellow believers. Ecclesiastes 4:11 well raises the question: "How can one be warm alone?" A fire, in order to burn brightly, must be made up of a number of coals or a number of sticks. God has instituted Christian fellowship for the purpose of keeping the saints warm and alive to His things.

The story has often been told of a brother who stopped attending services, with plenty of cause for discontent, in his own judgment. A true pastor went to see him and found him at home with a cheery fire of coals in the fireplace. After greetings and preliminary remarks, the visitor took a white hot coal of fire, and with the tongs laid it on the hearth in front of the fire, by itself. About ten minutes later, when the coal had become cold and black, he picked it up with his bare hand, threw it back on the fire, got his hat, bade his host good night and went out, without another word. The sermon was as clear as day. When one gets away from association with other believers, one soon gets cold and dark and useless.

Paul enjoyed the fire, but he well knew the scriptural teaching that true Christianity consists not merely of enjoying privileges but also of shouldering responsibility. Do you? If you really want to enjoy the warmth of Christian love, how about contributing towards it? "Pick up sticks" is the slogan for happy Christian fellowship. Paul gathered a bundle of sticks. He did not think himself above a little hard work—to scout around for wood to keep the fire going. It is hard and humble work, this stooping so low to pick up sticks.

Humble service; that is what God wants and what the saints need. There are plenty who want to have an office; not so many who want to do the work. Paul was not of that kind. He gathered a bundle (the Greek word is *multitude*) of sticks; he worked hard and brought a big load of wood. Remember too that it was raining, so it was no pleasant job. Many saints get discouraged easily when a little cold water is poured on their efforts; but not Paul. And the very work of gathering the wood would warm Paul as well. *Do* something for the Lord instead of sitting shivering and criticizing and you'll get warm and will warm others.

The devil does not like a happy, useful Christian. So— a viper came out of the heat and bit the apostle. Heat wakes snakes, I am told; it certainly rouses the devil.

When believers are cold or asleep, the devil goes to sleep too; no need to stand guard then. But let the Lord wake up His saints, let them get hot, and the devil is right there.

These heathen had the wrong idea, as do so many now who ought to know better. They decided Paul must have been a criminal because this poisonous serpent bit him. The reverse was true. The Bible shows clearly that Satan goes after those who walk closest to the Lord. The devil hates those whose lives and whose ministry exalt Christ; he ever will seek to hinder or harm them.

Paul shook off the beast into the fire. Many times believers are not so wise. They allow Satan to defeat them, instead of vice versa. When the devil sees a company of believers get on well, when God is working and souls are being saved, then he comes in to work his wiles. One of the most common and the most dreadful is to incite the saints to self-seeking and pride. These heathen looked for either one of two results in Paul's case: to see him swell up or to see him drop dead. Sinners fall down dead through Satan's lies and deceptions; believers are apt to swell up—with pride. How the devil loves to see a swelled head; how a Christian should shun it like the plague! But Paul wouldn't do either. There was no pride in him, so to speak, though we read that God sent the messenger of Satan to buffet him, lest he should be exalted above words; in other words, lest he should swell up with pride. God in His infinite mercy gave His faithful servant some affliction to keep him ever humble. If Paul needed to be kept from that curse of pride, how much more do we.

Paul shook off the beast. He refused the temptation, as it were. Into the fire the snake went. Satan and all his ways should be unsparingly rejected and refused by the believer. When Paul failed to fall dead or swell up, the natives changed their minds and said that he was a god. He was not, but the grace of God does enable the believer to live godlike in this present evil world!

Let us all learn these precious lessons from this incident. Let us keep the fire burning brightly, warming our own hearts, and attracting others to our precious Lord!